D1547867

The
STAR BOOK
on
PREACHING

Marvin A. McMickle

JUDSON PRESS
PUBLISHERS SINCE 1824
VALLEY FORGE

THE STAR BOOK ON PREACHING

© 2006 by Judson Press, Valley Forge, PA 19482-0851

Library of Congress Cataloging-in-Publication Data
McMickle, Marvin Andrew.
The star book on preaching / Marvin A. McMickle.
p. cm.
ISBN 0-8170-1492-6 (alk. paper)
1. Preaching. I. Title.
BV4211.3.M38 2006
251--dc22   2006003121

Printed in the U.S.A.

Third Printing, 2014.

Contents

Introduction

In my first course on public speaking in 1966, Asa Colby at Aurora College introduced me to this idea:

> If we want to learn to speak in public, let us start at the beginning. There is too much public speaking already. Much of it is trite, dull, boring or simply worthless. There is no justifiable place for that type of speaking. There is a place only for speaking that is worth listening to; and public speaking is not worth listening to unless it delivers useful goods to the listener.[1]

Forty years have passed since I took that first course in public speaking. From the perspective of those four intervening decades, three during which I have been preaching, reading, and hearing sermons, I have reached a similar conclusion about preaching. Too much of what is labeled as preaching is trite, dull, boring, or simply worthless. There is no justifiable place for that type of preaching. There is a place only for preaching that is worth listening to. And preaching is not worth listening to unless it "delivers useful goods" to the listener.

I hope in this book to set forth an approach to preaching that concentrates on enhancing a preacher's ability to "deliver the goods to the listener." The "goods" is the gospel of Jesus Christ. The "goods" is God's work of salvation. The "goods" is the greatest story ever told. This is what the world so desperately needs to hear. It is the message that God has entrusted to those of us who stand on a regular basis to preach a sermon to an assembled congregation or to a passing crowd on a busy street corner. Every time we preach we need to be sure we are "delivering the goods" to the listener.

Section I focuses on the preacher's call to duty. We need a theological understanding of the message we preach and the role we play in taking this message to the world. Section II reviews the lifestyle and study habits that can assist the preacher with personal spiritual formation so that preaching emerges from a full cup and a fresh spirit. Section III focuses on the goals and desired outcomes in preaching and on the methods that help guarantee that we are delivering the goods to the listener. Section IV concentrates on various sermonic forms that help us preach the gospel in a postmodern culture where the authority of Scripture and the authority of the preacher can no longer be assumed. Section V deals with some of the nuts and bolts aspects of sermon design and delivery. Section VI offers suggestions on why and how to make use of a sermon series. Section VII consists of eleven sermon outlines that point to the benefits of using the lectionary or some other method of text and topic selection. The book ends with a bibliography that may prove helpful in guiding preachers both in terms of which books to consult in their sermon preparation and which books they may want to purchase.

I have been preaching since I was sixteen. Through four decades as pastor and professor of preaching, I have tried to learn all I could about preaching so I could one day write a book on the topic. This is that book; I hope it "delivers the goods" to the reader.

Note
1. Excerpted from William Norwood Brigance, *Speech Communication* (New York: F. S. Crofts & Co., 1947), 1.

S E C T I O N   I

The Biblical Basis for Preaching

In the presence of God and of Christ Jesus, who will judge the living and the dead, and in view of his appearing and his kingdom, I give you this charge: Preach the Word; be prepared in season and out of season; correct, rebuke and encourage—with great patience and careful instruction.

—2 Timothy 4:1-2, NIV

What is preaching? Definitions abound for the work done by a person who stands to declare a word from the Lord. Preaching is not an invention of the modern world. Preaching did not begin with Martin Luther in the Protestant Reformation. Preaching is not a gift to us from Aristotle and his reflections on rhetoric. Preaching is the method by which God has chosen to communicate his will and ways to the world. In fact, before we get to definitions of preaching or talk about sermon design, it might be best to establish preaching as an action that comes with authority and significance because it is an act that is firmly and deeply rooted in the biblical record.

No passage in the Bible offers a better avenue into an understanding of preaching as a biblical act than 2 Timothy 4:1-2. These words from Paul to Timothy set forth the clearest and most compelling case for the biblical basis of and authority for preaching. The text begins with Paul calling Timothy to the task of preaching. He was doing so not by his own authority alone, but also in the name and authority of God and Christ Jesus. This Scripture reminds us that preaching is not meant to be done by volunteers who believe that they have what it takes to succeed. Preaching is less a *profession* to be chosen and more a *professing*—of truths God has placed upon a person's heart and of teachings from which that person cannot turn away.

1. Called to Preach

"I solemnly urge you," Paul told Timothy—or as the New King James Version puts it, "I charge you." Preaching is best done under *compulsion*, under *conviction*, and under *constraint*. No one knew this any better than Paul himself when he cried out, "I am compelled to preach. Woe to me if I do not preach the gospel" (1 Corinthians 9:16, NIV). The prophet Jeremiah felt an equal sense of conviction about preaching when he said, "If I say, 'I will not mention him, or speak any more in his name,' then within me there is something like a burning fire shut up in my bones; I am weary with holding it in, and I cannot" (Jeremiah 20:9).

The same could be said about Peter and John, who were arrested by the religious leaders in Jerusalem and offered release on the single condition that they no longer speak about Jesus. The apostles refused and justified their continued preaching by saying, "Whether it is right in God's sight to listen to you rather than to God, you must judge; for we cannot keep from speaking about what we have seen and heard" (Acts 4:19-20).

Paul reinforced the importance of a call to preach in his letter to the church in Rome when he linked the salvation of the world to the work of preaching. He began by saying that "everyone who calls on the name of the Lord shall be saved" (Romans 10:13). Then he worked his way back from the finished task of salvation to the process by which it is accomplished. "But how are they to call on one in whom they have not believed? And how are they to believe in one of whom they have never heard? And how are they to hear without someone to proclaim him? And how are they to proclaim him unless they are sent?" (Romans 10:14-15).

Preaching in the Old Testament

Paul's challenge to Timothy to "preach the word" was by no means the first time such a call to preach had been issued, nor would it be the first time that preaching the word of God would take place as part of God's salvation plan. The first call to preach came on the backside of Mt. Horeb when God called Moses out of a burning bush (see Exodus 3:1-10), and the first sermon was delivered when God sent Moses back to Egypt to tell Pharaoh to let God's people go free (Exodus 5). The biblical prophets began their oracles by saying, "Thus says the LORD" (see Amos 1:3) or "the spirit of the LORD God is upon me" (Isaiah 61:1) or "For thus the LORD, the God of Israel, said to me" (Jeremiah 25:15). In each case the prophet was declaring the fact that what he was speaking came from God, and he was delivering it to whomever God intended to hear. Each of these prophets was called to preach the word of God.

Preaching in the New Testament

The New Testament is alive with the power of preaching. The Gospel of Matthew describes John the Baptist's preaching debut with these words: "In those days John the Baptist appeared in the wilderness of Judea, proclaiming, 'Repent, for the kingdom of heaven has come near'" (Matthew 3:1-2). In the same chapter that Mark's Gospel describes John's preaching ministry, Jesus also appears, and his entrance is announced by the words, "Jesus came to Galilee, proclaiming the good news of God" (Mark 1:14). In Matthew 11:1, the emphasis on preaching continues as Scripture describes Jesus by saying, "he went on from there to teach and proclaim his message in their cities." One of those preaching events is described in Mark 2:1-2 when Jesus was in a home in Capernaum: "So many gathered around that there was no longer room for them, not even in front of the door; and he was speaking the word to them."

Jesus gave a charge to his disciples to preach the word in Matthew 10:7, Mark 6:7-13, and Luke 9:1-6. In each case, Scripture makes clear that Jesus was calling his disciples to preach the gospel as he had taught it to them, and as he himself had done. That call to preach was issued by Jesus to his disciples even more definitively in the Great Commission passages:

> Jesus came and said to them, "All authority in heaven and on earth has been given to me. Go therefore and make disciples of all nations, baptizing them in the name of the Father and of the Son and of the Holy Spirit, and teaching them to obey everything that I have commanded you. And remember, I am with you always, to the end of the age." (Matthew 28:18-20)

> And he said to them, "Go into all the world and proclaim the good news to the whole creation. The one who believes and is baptized will be

saved; but the one who does not believe will be condemned. . . ." And they went out and proclaimed the good news everywhere, while the Lord worked with them and confirmed the message by the signs that accompanied it. (Mark 16:15-16, 20)

Preaching in the Early Church

Preaching was a central component for the early church. Peter, who had earlier denied even knowing who Jesus was, preached his first sermon on the Day of Pentecost, and three thousand souls were added to the church that day (Acts 2:14-42). The disciples continued to preach in Jerusalem, as evidenced by these words: "And every day in the temple and at home they did not cease to teach and proclaim Jesus as the Messiah" (Acts 5:42). The office and work of the *diaconate* (deacon) was created to relieve the apostles of certain administrative duties so, as Peter said, "We, for our part, will devote ourselves to prayer and to serving the word" (Acts 6:4).

Following his conversion, Paul made three missionary journeys throughout the Mediterranean world, and preaching was central to each of them. Paul and Barnabas preached in Cyprus, Antioch, and other cities. Paul and Silas preached in Philippi, Athens, Corinth, and Ephesus, among other places. Even after he was arrested, Paul continued to preach, first to a mob in the temple (Acts 21:37–22:21), then before the Sanhedrin (Acts 23:1-11), and eventually before the Roman official Felix (Acts 24:10-21). Finally, in one of the most dramatic moments in his ministry, Paul preached before the Roman governor Festus and King Agrippa. Paul preached with such passion and conviction that Festus declared, "You are out of your mind, Paul! Too much learning is driving you insane!" (Acts 26:24). The response of King Agrippa was even more memorable, for he declared, "Are you so quickly persuading me to become a Christian?" (Acts 26:28).

Preaching is central to the epistles of Peter and John as well. In his first letter, the apostle Peter delivered a lesson about salvation and discipleship that he ends by saying, "That word is the good news that was announced ["preached," NIV] to you" (1 Peter 1:25). In his subsequent correspondence, Peter referred to preaching when he said, "Therefore I intend to keep on reminding you of these things, though you know them already and are established in the truth that has come to you. I think it right, as long as I am in this body, to refresh your memory" (2 Peter 1:12-13).

John's first epistle begins with a fervent affirmation of preaching:

> We declare to you what was from the beginning, what we have heard, what we have seen with our

eyes, what we have looked at and touched with our hands, concerning the word of life. . . . This is the message we have heard from him and proclaim to you, that God is light and in him there is no darkness at all. (1 John 1:1, 5)

Preaching throughout the Biblical Story

It ought to be clear by now that preaching is the thread that ties the biblical epoch together. The entire salvation story is punctuated by preaching. The word of God went forth with power and purpose from the gilded palace of Pharaoh to the windswept, desolate prison colony of Patmos. Preaching was the means by which God communicated his will to kings and nations, to Israel and Assyria, to Greece and Rome, from the twelfth century B.C. until the biblical story comes to an end at the close of the first century A.D. The Bible is the record of preaching that took place over a period of thirteen hundred years. More important, this same practice of preaching has continued to this very day, and the words of Romans 10:15 remain true for those who are the preachers of the twenty-first century: "How beautiful are the feet of those who bring good news!"

2. Preach the Word

Second Timothy 4:1-2 further establishes the *content* of our preaching. Paul not only charged Timothy to engage in the act of preaching, but he established for his young protégé the content that should fill his sermons: "Preach the word." Timothy was not being called to preach his own opinions or to echo the opinions of the culture around him. Timothy was charged with preaching the gospel of Jesus Christ. He was to recount the meaning of the life of Jesus and to preach that "in Christ God was reconciling the world to himself" (2 Corinthians 5:19). Timothy was to reflect upon the death of Jesus on the cross and say, "While we were still weak, at the right time Christ died for the ungodly. . . . But God proves his love for us in that while we still were sinners Christ died for us" (Romans 5:6, 8). Timothy was to underscore the importance of the resurrection of Jesus by declaring, "But in fact Christ has been raised from the dead, the first fruits of those who have died. For since death came through a human being, the resurrection of the dead has also come through a human being" (1 Corinthians 15:20-21). Thus, the first responsibility of any preacher is to preach the Word.

Commit to Preaching the Word

Throughout his own ministry, Paul avoided needless controversies and petty squabbles by concentrating his energies on preaching the Word. In 1 Corinthians 1:7 he wrote, "For Christ did not send me to baptize but to proclaim the gospel, and not with eloquent wisdom, so that the cross of Christ might not be emptied of its power." In that same letter he wrote these words: "I decided to know nothing among you except Jesus Christ, and him crucified" (1 Corinthians 2:2). So intent was Paul on keeping the church focused on the gospel he was preaching that he told the church in Galatia to listen to no other message but his. He wrote, "But even if we or an angel from heaven should proclaim to you a gospel contrary to what we proclaimed to you, let that one be accursed! As we have said before, so now I repeat, if anyone proclaims to you a gospel contrary to what you received, let that one be accursed!" (Galatians 1:8-9).

To his apprentice Timothy, Paul advocated a similar message, only this time focusing almost entirely on the content of the message: the Scriptures. In his second letter to his spiritual son, Paul wrote:

> But as for you, continue in what you have learned and firmly believed, knowing from whom you learned it, and how from childhood you have known the sacred writings that are able to instruct you for salvation through faith in Christ Jesus. All scripture is inspired by God and is useful for teaching, for reproof, for correction, and for training in righteousness, so that everyone

who belongs to God may be proficient, equipped
for every good work. (2 Timothy 3:14-17)

Commit to Sound Doctrine

The best way for preachers to preach the word is to
pay attention to what Paul called "sound doctrine." In
fact, this was a recurring theme in the apostle's writings
to Timothy. In 1 Timothy 1:10-11, Paul spoke of "the
sound teaching ["doctrine," NIV] that conforms to the
glorious gospel of the blessed God, which he entrusted
to me." In that same letter, he wrote, "Watch your life
and doctrine closely. Persevere in them, because if
you do, you will save both yourself and your hearers"
(1 Timothy 4:16, NIV). In his second letter, Paul again
reminded Timothy that preaching must be done with
great patience and in accordance with sound doctrine
(see 2 Timothy 4:1-5). People may not understand the
message the first time they hear it, so the preacher must
continue to preach the doctrines of the church.

The basis of sound doctrine is found in the Scriptures
themselves. Therefore, Paul told Timothy, "Do your
best to present yourself to God as one approved
by him, a worker who has no need to be ashamed,
rightly explaining the word of truth" (2 Timothy 2:15).
At a time when people were saying that in order to
become a Christian you would first have to become
a circumcised follower of the laws of Moses, Paul

understood the importance of sound doctrine. At a time when Gentile converts might still be intrigued by Greek philosophy or Gnosticism or the belief in many gods (as Paul encountered in Athens; see Acts 17), there was a need for sound doctrine.

In his classic book *Apostolic Preaching*, C. H. Dodd reminded modern preachers of the central role that the *kerygma* played in the preaching content of the early church. The *kerygma* constituted the central doctrines of the Christian faith. No early Christian preacher who failed to pay attention to these doctrines could be considered faithful. That principle has not changed. This means that our preaching also must touch upon the themes and texts dealing with the incarnation of Jesus; his mission, miracles, and ministry; his passion (arrest, suffering, and death on the cross) and resurrection; as well as on the mission and ministry of the church in the world for purposes of evangelism and on eschatology, which comprises reflections on the end time that is marked by the second coming of Christ.

Any number of issues and events can too easily serve as a substitute for attention to sound doctrine in preaching. It may well be that contemporary issues can best be discussed and analyzed as we consider them through the lens of the major doctrines of the faith. However, we cannot allow our preaching to be determined *solely* by the headlines of the newspaper or the most recent events in our community. What we can and should do is attempt to bring some *kerygmatic* perspective to these events and headlines. This is best accomplished when we adhere to sound doctrine as our major focus. We ought to pay attention to Psalm 119:105, which says, "Your word is a lamp to my feet and a light to my path." As we consider any contemporary issue or event from the perspective of biblical teaching and sound doctrine, we will have the benefit of enlightenment that only God can provide.

3. Be Prepared

There are high and low times in the life of the preacher. The next lesson we glean from Paul's advice to Timothy is a reminder to be prepared to preach in a variety of settings, under a variety of conditions, before a variety of audiences, and on a variety of themes and topics. Paul was his student of something that the apostle himself had undoubtedly discovered during his long and arduous ministry, namely, that the word must be declared whether the preacher feels like doing so or not. Not every day will find the preacher full of energy and enthusiasm for the task ahead, but the preacher must declare the Word of the Lord nevertheless.

There will be Sundays when a preacher cannot wait to reach the pulpit to share the message for that day. The preacher may feel particularly inspired, and the message may be especially encouraging for the waiting congregation. This is "in season" preaching. There will also be, however, other Sundays when the preacher feels hesitant about the text, when the message is hard to speak and even harder to receive. Even in these "out-of-season" moments, the word must be declared. Occasionally preaching will need to address themes the congregation does not want to hear discussed from the pulpit, themes the people wish the preacher would just leave alone. That is one application of being prepared in season and out of season. Be prepared when they want to hear you and when they do not want to hear you, at least not on that subject.

Preach in the Sanctuary and Beyond

Not every sermon will be preached in the sanctuary. Paul's advice to Timothy extends to preachers today, adjuring us to know that not every sermon will or *should* be delivered in the safety and serenity of a sanctuary, a chapel, or even a tent at an open-air revival. There will be those times when the preacher must declare the Word in some out-of-season locations, at least so far as the preacher's comfort and the congregation's expectations are concerned. The ministries of Paul and Jesus reflect this very point. They could be found preaching on city streets, on mountainsides, at social gatherings, in jails and prisons, and in the presence of political leaders who were hostile to their message.

The same must be true for all preachers. On some days, our pulpit may be the steps of City Hall. A message from God may be in order at a political demonstration for fair wages, for an end to war, or in opposition to an unjust international trade policy. People may not be expecting a sermon at times such as these, but a word from the Lord may be just what is needed.

A sermon on such occasions may not be designed to win converts as much as to give voice to the broad themes of justice, compassion, and peace that run throughout the Bible. The sermon might not even be structured in any homiletic form that marks the usual Sunday morning sermon. What is most important in times and places like these is not the style but the substance, "not the manner but the matter," as Gardner C. Taylor has so often observed. In accepting the call to preach, you are committing to be prepared, in season and out of season.

Preach to All People

The Bible is full of reminders that preachers should prepare themselves early on in ministry to preach before a wide variety of audiences in a wide variety of physical settings. One week might find the preacher inside the barbed wire of a maximum-security prison, preaching a word that is helpful to those who live and work there together, both inmates and employees alike. Another week might find the same preacher visiting a senior citizens' center and ministering among the residents, and later joining a group of teenagers gathered around a campfire. We should not be so specialized in our approach to preaching that we are effective with only one kind of audience. *Be prepared.*

Like Paul and Jesus, who preached before a wide variety of audiences, we should be prepared for the challenges of changing contexts with *corresponding changes in content.* When Jesus preached in the synagogues, he started with a text from the holy Scriptures (see Luke 4). When he spoke to the crowds who followed him, he spun them a story, a parable (see Luke 15). Paul employed similar strategies in his ministry, tailoring his presentation and approach to the audience he addressed. He went so far as to declare:

> To the Jews I became as a Jew, in order to win Jews. To those under the law I became as one under the law . . . so that I might win those under the law. To those outside the law I became as one outside the law . . . so that I might win those outside the law. To the weak I became weak, so that I might win the weak. I have become all things to all people, that I might by all means save some. (1 Corinthians 9:20-22)

It is very likely that the gospel would never have taken root if Jesus and Paul had limited themselves to preaching only before the standard synagogue crowds of Jerusalem and Antioch and Ephesus and Athens. It is just as likely that if we want the gospel to extend to the ends of the earth, then we had better be prepared to preach beyond our sanctuaries. Just as Jeremiah preached in the streets of Jerusalem and Jonah preached in the streets of Nineveh, so must preachers today be prepared to take their message beyond their local churches and into the out-of-season regions of the world.

4. Correct, Rebuke, and Encourage

Sometimes we must preach an out-of-season message in an in-season location. One of the great tests of a preacher is the extent to which he or she is prepared to speak a hard or critical or correcting word to the congregation with whom the preacher has a continuing relationship. Part of Paul's challenge in 2 Timothy 4:1-4 was the understanding that not every sermon can be a "welcomed word." Sometimes we must preach words that our people do not want to hear, and we must do it as much for our own sake as for theirs. Like the prophet called to be a watchman in Ezekiel 33:1-9, we may see our people behaving in ways that are contrary to the will of God, and if we fail to warn them, God will hold us responsible. Therefore, a preacher must develop the ability to vary the themes and purposes of the sermon so that those who hear sermons over a period of time will be *corrected, rebuked,* and *encouraged* in the appropriate seasons.

Jesus Is Our Role Model

The best illustration of preaching that corrects, rebukes, and also encourages may be the sermon preached by Jesus in the synagogue in Nazareth as recorded in Luke 4:14-30. This passage is important, first of all because it establishes the *format* in which most of our preaching will take place. Jesus came to the synagogue (a certain place) on the Sabbath (a certain day), read out of the scroll of Isaiah (a certain book), and then commented upon what he read (a certain action). This is the essence of preaching to this day: A person comes to a church on the Lord's Day to hear a message based on a reading from the Scriptures. In this single passage, Jesus established a pattern that his followers have used ever since.

However, the point of interest in this text is not merely the format but the *content* of what Jesus had to say to that crowd. First there was a word of instruction, perhaps even of revelation, as Jesus announced that the messianic promises mentioned in Isaiah 61 had been fulfilled by his own appearance. The crowd in Nazareth received this message surprisingly well, considering that a young man who had grown up in their village and had probably had his bar mitzvah in that very synagogue was now declaring himself to be the Messiah.

The things Jesus said next were not so well received. Jesus went on to declare that the love of God was not limited to the nation of Israel. He observed that in the days of Elijah, God's love extended to a woman from Phoenicia and in the days of Elisha, God's love extended to a man from Syria. This was, in essence, a rebuke, a corrective to the long-held belief that the people of Israel were the sole beneficiaries of Yahweh's love and affection. Not so, said Jesus, and in response to that message, the people in the synagogue became enraged and attempted to throw him to his death off a cliff. People in those days did not like to be rebuked or corrected; they do not like it much more today.

Other Biblical Examples

The Bible offers many examples of preaching, but the fact is, preaching in the Bible was seldom met with a warm response. That may be a result of the fact that the prophets, the judges, the apostles, and Jesus himself were doing the hard work of correcting and rebuking as much as they offered words of encouragement. The words of Moses were repeatedly ignored by Pharaoh (Exodus 5–11). King Zedekiah imprisoned Jeremiah for speaking an out-of-season word (Jeremiah 32:2-3). The preaching of John the Baptist ultimately cost that prophet his head (Mark 6:14-29). The preaching of Jesus earned him a place on the cross. Paul was beheaded, and John was imprisoned. All of these things happened because these early preachers were willing to engage in the unsettling and often unpopular business of preaching messages that corrected and rebuked.

Of course, reminders such as these may be precisely why so many preachers shy away from sermons that correct or rebuke; they do not want to face any negative consequences from their pulpit work. Preachers may be enamored of the idea that every Sunday morning ought to find the entire congregation filing past them at the end of the service and saying, "What a wonderful sermon, Pastor. We so much enjoyed what you had to say." A better gauge might be those occasional Sundays when people exit by another door, refusing to shake the preacher's hand because the sermon was as disturbing to them as the one preached by Jesus in the synagogue at Nazareth.

Different Purposes at Different Times

The Bible sets before us the reminder that preaching must serve many purposes over the course of time. There are moments when a word of encouragement is needed, including in times of death or sickness or distress. There are times when the best thing we can say to someone from the word of God is "underneath are the everlasting arms" (Deuteronomy 33:27, NIV). That is good *pastoral* preaching.

However, there are other times when our preaching must engage in what Robert McCracken calls "disturbing the conscience." This is the example set before us by many of those whose preaching we read in the pages of Scripture. As much as preachers might like to be affirmed by their congregation every Sunday, we need to heed the words of Jesus in Luke 6:26: "Woe to you when all speak well of you, for that is what their ancestors did to the false prophets."

Different Preachers, Different Ministries

The last lesson we should extract from 2 Timothy 4:1-2 is that not all preachers are called by God to engage in the same kind of ministry. Paul was an apostle to the Gentiles, and his ministry was to carry the gospel to those people and places that the name of Jesus had never penetrated. This was the ministry whose completion he was celebrating when he wrote in 2 Timothy 4:7, "I have fought the good fight, I have finished the race, I have kept the faith." Now Paul was challenging Timothy to assume the duties that God was going to assign to him. Paul was not naming a successor; he was ordaining a son and urging him to go out and find his own voice and his own ministry.

Paul's words in Ephesians 4:11-12 remind us that different preachers are called to follow different courses, albeit all in pursuit of the same goal in the end: "The gifts he gave were that some would be apostles, some prophets, some evangelists, some pastors and teachers, to equip the saints for the work of ministry, for building up the body of Christ. . . ." The Bible challenges every preacher to "confirm your call and election" (2 Peter 1:10). Peter's ministry was not the same as that of Paul. John the Baptist played a role very different from that of Jesus. Matthias was elected to replace Judas in the ranks of the original apostles (Acts 1:15-26), and although he never seemed to achieve the renown of James or John, from what traditions tells us, he accomplished the ministry to which he had been assigned.

In short, not only does the Bible provide us with the basis for the content and context of our preaching, but Scripture also provides us with a way to discern the contours of the ministry in which each of us should be engaged. Some may preach to great congregations and before national audiences. Others may operate at a less visible level, pouring out their hearts to a local church. Some may plant new churches with fifty to one hundred souls participating, while others may preach to thousands at a time. Whatever the circumstances, the same message applies: "Preach the word."

SECTION II

The Heart and Habits of the Preacher

The apostles gathered around Jesus, and told him all that they had done and taught. He said to them, "Come away to a deserted place all by yourselves and rest a while." For many were coming and going, and they had no leisure even to eat. And they went away in the boat to a deserted place by themselves. Now many saw them going and recognized them, and they hurried there on foot from all the towns and arrived ahead of them. As he went ashore, he saw a great crowd; and he had compassion for them, because they were like sheep without a shepherd; and he began to teach them many things.

—Mark 6:30-34

The life of an active pastor and preacher is vividly captured in an encounter between Jesus and his disciples in Mark 6:30-34. The disciples had just returned from their first preaching mission after Jesus had sent them out two by two. They had ministered in various locations, and now they had reunited and were eager to report to Jesus all they had done. However, they could not reflect on their experiences because, even though they had just finished one very exhausting task, a crowd of people had already gathered around them with something else for them to do. So intense was their work schedule that they "did not have a chance to eat" (NIV).

Rather than allow them to get caught up in another cycle of work right on the heels of the mission they had just completed, Jesus stepped in and invited them to join him on a short retreat where they could rest, regroup, and then reflect on their preaching mission. Jesus said to them, "Come with me by yourselves to a quiet place and get some rest" (NIV). Jesus was inviting his first group of disciples to take a little time off, get away from the job, be refreshed and renewed, and then go back to face the work again on another day.

As the biblical text makes clear, the retreat Jesus was trying to schedule proved to be harder to achieve than he planned (see vv. 33-34). Jesus and the disciples got into a boat and sailed to a solitary place in an attempt to get away from the crowds, away from the pressures of their ministry. However, people saw them boarding the boat and followed them to the place they were headed. The crowd did not care that the disciples had just finished a grueling mission around the country. The crowd did not care that Jesus and his disciples might be tired and in need of a few days away from their work. The crowd saw where the disciples were going, and the people followed them. Jesus seemed to know (and the disciples would soon find out) that the people they served in ministry would not leave them alone even when the disciples tried to get away for a break.

This story speaks pointedly to the schedule that most pastors and preachers maintain on a regular basis. No sooner have we completed one task than there is another one awaiting us. No sooner have we finished the Sunday morning service than it is time to work on the sermon for a funeral on Tuesday. No sooner is the funeral over than it is time to get ready for the Wednesday evening Bible study. No sooner is that over than committees, boards, denominational agencies, and civic responsibilities clamor for our attention. If preachers are to be able to serve effectively in the present moment and to survive the pace and pressure of the career path we have chosen, we must heed the words of Jesus to his first disciples: "Come with me by yourselves to a quiet place and get some rest."

Time management is as important a skill for the preacher as exegesis. One of our most important resources as preachers is time. We receive it in limited amounts and must be careful to make maximum use out of every second. However, this does not mean that we should be workaholics who look upon vacations and retreats as a waste of time or as a sign that we are less than faithful to our calling. Instead, preachers need to see times of rest and retreat and renewal as being absolutely essential for a healthy body and for a successful, long-term ministry. This passage in Mark 6 should not be ignored, because Jesus was inviting his disciples to establish a habit of pastoral self-care. It was a habit that Jesus practiced himself throughout his ministry. Luke 5:16 observes that as the news about Jesus' powerful ministry spread, the crowds would actively pursue him, "but he would withdraw to deserted places to pray" (see also Matthew 14:23; Mark 6:46; Luke 6:12). It is a habit of self-care that any and all who seek to serve in Christ's name should emulate. As one of my parishioners in Montclair, New Jersey, told me more than twenty-five years ago, "Come apart before you fall apart."

1. Take Time for Your Health

The first thing active preachers and pastors must do is take some time away from the job to take care of their health. Take time to walk or to engage in a favorite pastime that gets your heart pumping and your mind off of the work of ministry. Take time for an annual medical examination, and then take time to follow up on any recommendations from your physician. In the course of even the busiest days in ministry, take time to eat properly and maintain good nutrition. A fast-paced life should not become dependent on a fast-food diet. While a hamburger and fries might sound inviting, a fruit salad or a grilled chicken sandwich on wheat would be a better choice. No matter how great your zeal for ministry, there is not much you can do for the kingdom of God if you are sick or exhausted or on the verge of a stroke all the time because of a sedentary lifestyle complicated by a bad diet. Take time to maintain good health.

Get Some Rest

In the 1958 film *The Ten Commandments*, Rameses II (played by Yul Brenner) questions Moses (played by Charlton Heston) about his reason for giving the Hebrew slaves one day a week to rest from their labor of making bricks for the monuments and palaces of Egypt. Moses provides a practical answer for his labor policies, one that preachers and pastors would do well to remember. Moses tells his brother, "The strong make many bricks, the weak make few, and the dead make none!" Moses was not being soft or benevolent so much as he was being practical and realistic. Nobody can work all the time without negative effects sooner or later. "Come apart by yourselves and get some rest."

Get Away from It All

Preachers should take time for vacations where we can get away from the pressures of the job. And a week spent at a church convention where you are up to your neck in denominational meetings and conferences should not be considered a vacation. In fact, most of us need a vacation *after* attending our denomination's annual or biennial gathering. What each of us does and where we choose to go to enjoy a vacation is a matter of personal choice. However, it is a universal truth that all preachers need to get away from the office, the pulpit, and the people for a period of time that allows us to be refreshed and reinvigorated.

Jesus did this on a regular basis. He would go up into the mountains to be alone. He would even send his own disciples away for a while so he could spend some time apart from them. This time away from the job should not be viewed as "wasted time." No matter how busy we are with our ministry, we must heed the lessons of Mark 6 and take care of our health.

2. Take Time for Your Head

Would you be willing to place your life in the hands of a surgeon who had graduated from medical school fifteen years ago and who had not read an article or received any additional training in his or her specialty since that time? Would you have much confidence in a lawyer who was not familiar with the most recent rulings from the United States Supreme Court or from the regulatory agencies that oversee the area of business in which that lawyer is charging $200 per hour to advise clients? Absolutely not! We expect and demand that those professionals who serve us be on the cutting edge of information and expertise in their practice. We expect them to be involved in a steady regimen of continuing education.

Those who hear our sermons should expect and receive no less from us. We should take some time away from our work in order to update and improve the work that we do. This can mean a daily discipline of reading professional journals, newspapers, and news magazines to keep current on the issues affecting the church, the community, and the world. It may include studying books dealing with biblical interpretation and theology, as well as books that offer the newest ideas and insights in sermon design and delivery. It can also mean time away at workshops and conferences where we can be challenged by scholars and creative thinkers who can awaken new energy and enthusiasm for the work we do.

Know Your Scriptures

A lack of knowledge can lead to embarrassing consequences. I remember sitting on the platform of a church next to a young minister who had been asked by the host pastor to read the passage from 2 Chronicles. It was sad to watch him searching for 2 Chronicles somewhere among the epistles of Paul and then within the body of books that make up the prophets. Finally, he turned to the index section to find the page on which the book of 2 Chronicles began. All of this was done in clear view of the more than two thousand people who were seated in the congregation for that occasion.

Time spent with Scripture familiarizes us not only with its content, but also with its "geography." Nothing is worse than when a preacher, whose primary resource is the biblical text, makes a home or hospital visit and is asked to read to a distressed or grieving person from a book of the Bible the preacher cannot easily locate or perhaps cannot find at all! Take time with Scripture as a way to strengthen your own spiritual foundations, but also to increase your knowledge.

Add to Your Knowledge

Continuing education is an excellent way to take time for your head. You can accomplish this by taking courses at a nearby seminary, university, or even a community college. You might even decide to pursue an advanced degree in theology or some related field. Whatever you decide to do, be sure that you get involved in something that gets you away from the hectic schedule of your work long enough to update your existing skills and maybe even learn some new ones.

Consider taking a course in a presentation software, such as Microsoft's PowerPoint, so you can add some twenty-first-century technology to your worship service and pulpit presentations. People who work on a job where technology is an everyday reality will not be surprised or disturbed if they see it being used in their church.

If your church is located in an area with a growing Hispanic presence, take a language course or borrow a book or audiotapes from the library to learn some basic Spanish. Doing the same would be advisable if your community has a substantial population of any non-English speakers. Taking time to learn the language and the culture of your neighborhood is a wise and strategic investment related to the evangelism mission of your congregation.

Grow in the Spirit

Subscribe to journals such as *Preaching*, *The African American Pulpit*, *The Living Pulpit*, and *Interpretation*. Stay current on events in the life of the church universal and society in general through news magazines such as *Christian Century* and *Christianity Today*. These magazines not only provide important articles and interviews that can enrich the life and work of any preacher, but they also provide invaluable book reviews that can aid a cash-strapped preacher in making the best use of his or her resources.

I cannot stress enough that this investment of time and money should not be made simply in preparation for a sermon. These disciplines should be engaged in because they are an essential part of the ongoing preparation of the preacher.

During the Colonial period in this country, the pastor was generally considered one of the best educated and most widely read members of the community. That is no longer the typical perception of clergy among many within society today, but this is more our own fault than anyone else's. It is simply a matter of "coming apart" for a while.

3. Take Time for Your Home

Scripture makes a statement that is sadly true of far too many pastors and preachers: "[They] made me take care of the vineyards; my own vineyard I have neglected" (Song of Songs of 1:6, NIV). More than a few preachers are so busy caring for the needs of others in the congregation that they fail to allot enough time to care for the needs within their own home. Slow down long enough to call a friend across town or a child or sibling living somewhere across the country. In the age of the Internet and e-mail, this is much easier to do, and we should do it more often. Time spent with your family and friends is vitally important for the development of a well-balanced life.

Manage Your Own Household

If you are married, take time to celebrate anniversaries and birthdays. If you have children, a band concert, a ballet recital, a football awards banquet, or a broken heart following the end of a relationship should be a matter fully deserving your attention. Getting involved in the life and routine of the home by sharing in the household chores, by maintaining a favorite room, or by assuming responsibility for planting or weeding or watering the flowers in the yard are among the ways you can be a part of the life of your home and family.

It is difficult if not impossible to have any authority when you decide to preach about marriage, child rearing, or the intergenerational challenges of family life when people know that you are not practicing what you preach. No matter how busy your day is, take the time to go home for dinner. At the very least, call home for a brief chat if you absolutely cannot return in time to share the evening meal. Carve out some time for a trip to the movies or the beach, or spend a leisurely afternoon sitting around the house. If you do not come apart from your work to spend time with your family, you might just see your family beginning to come apart.

Balance Home and Ministry

One of the reasons Roman Catholic priests and "religious women" (nuns) are unmarried is so they do not *have* to take time away from their family responsibilities to attend to their ministry duties. They can devote themselves entirely to their work. That was the rationale cited by the apostle Paul in 1 Corinthians 7:7-8, when he actually encouraged an unmarried and celibate lifestyle for the clergy leaders of the early church. However, the hallmark of the Protestant church has been the initial acceptance, (and now the norm) of a married clergy. The two—church family and domestic family—should be seen as going together. Time must be allotted for both, and neither should feel deprived because too much attention is being devoted to the other. Part of what Jesus was doing in Mark 6 was getting the disciples away from the crowd so they could have some private time among themselves. Take time for your home.

4. Take Time for Honesty

Be honest with yourself *about* yourself. Aristotle observed, "The unexamined life is not worth living." Not only should we be preaching that principle to others, but we should also be practicing it by doing a bit of self-examination ourselves. Take some time to be self-critical of the work you are doing. Only *you* really know how much time you are investing in your reading and your prayer life. Only *you* know how rushed or thorough your preparation for your next sermon has been. Only *you* know whether or not you really and truly believe and trust in the things you are asking others to believe and trust in when you preach.

Use Your Own Voice

Be sure you are preaching in your "own voice" and are not simply copying and mimicking the style and manner of some other preacher. As Shakespeare wrote in *Hamlet*, "This above all: to thine own self be true. And it must follow as the night the day that thou canst not be false to any man." No matter how impressed you are by the timbre of voice possessed by another preacher or the apparent success another leader seems to be enjoying in ministry, work hard to be true to yourself—to your own gifts and calling. No matter how successful others appear to be, do not blindly adopt their preaching practices and techniques in an attempt to create similar results in your ministry. God made them the way they are, and God made you the way you are. God did not make a mistake when he made you, but you can make a grave mistake if you turn your back on your natural gifts and mannerisms because you have become overly infatuated with the preaching style of someone else.

In our celebrity-conscious society, preachers are tempted to think they must have the prophetic edge of

Jesse Jackson or the zeal and passion of T. D. Jakes, the expositional skill of John McArthur or the wit and wisdom of Barbara Brown Taylor or Suzan Johnson Cook. Nothing could be further from the truth, because while God can use high profile preachers, God is equally needy of humble and little-known preachers who heed the warning of Mother Teresa, who said that God did not call us to be successful but to be faithful.

A Biblical Case Study

Mother Teresa's comment brings to mind the story in Acts 1:15-26, in which the apostles chose someone to fill the vacancy in their ranks created by the death of Judas, who killed himself after his betrayal of Jesus. A man named Matthias, who met every requirement for becoming an apostle and was nominated by Peter, was chosen to fill the vacancy. It is interesting to note that the name and contributions of Peter are known all over the world by Christians of all denominations and traditions. By contrast, how many people have ever heard of Matthias? There is no city, no hospital, no school, and only very few churches named in his honor.

Matthias did not strive to become like Peter, and he was never quoted as complaining about his low-profile status in the work of the kingdom of God. Even though he ran the same risks faced by the original disciples, and even though he probably died a martyr's death as did all the other apostles, Matthias served out his ministry in relative obscurity.

Not all preachers are called upon to preach at national conventions or to be published in preaching journals or to be listed among the "top preachers" in the country. Not all preachers are called to adopt the role of Peter; many are called and equipped to work on a smaller stage before a smaller audience. Preachers do well to serve faithfully in the place where God has set us and to use the gifts God has given us. That is far better than our trying to "walk like" a certain popular preacher or "dress like" some well-known TV evangelist or imitate the cadences or mannerisms of some nationally renowned pulpit giant.

Accept No Imitations

Gardner Taylor once spoke to this issue as a visiting lecturer in a preaching class when I was in seminary. He warned us that preachers who seek to imitate the style and manner of another preacher, particularly one of the nationally renowned preachers, will likely fail twice. They will fail the first time because they cannot truly become like the other person. After all, no one else can have access to that other person's life experiences, emotional makeup, or natural gifts and talents. They will fail a second time, Dr. Taylor observed, because in their haste to become like someone else, they will fail to become all that God intended and equipped *them* to be as preachers.

It is bad enough when preachers commit plagiarism and steal sermons from one another. It is worse when preachers commit "homiletical suicide" by abandoning our own style and substance in order to copy someone else's preaching style, voice, posture, theology, and sometimes even their manner of dress. Take some time to be sure that you are being true to yourself as God made and equipped you for the preaching ministry.

5. Take Time for Your Heart

I'm not talking here about cardiovascular health (although that is also important, as noted earlier in this chapter), but about spiritual health and how we as preachers need to take to heart the words of Psalm 119:11: "I treasure your word in my heart, so that I may not sin against you." Preachers need to spend quality time in the reading and study of Scripture, not merely in pursuit of our next sermon, but rather in pursuit of our own spiritual formation. We need to study the Word of God and internalize it so that it guides and directs our own lives as much as we hope it will guide and direct the lives of those to whom we preach.

Psalm 119:11 is translated vividly in the New International Version: "I have hidden your word in my heart. . . ." This image is to be contrasted with that of a preacher who is seen carrying a Bible around in the hand all the time but does not personally live by its teachings. Hiding the Word in your heart is to be contrasted with holding great amounts of Scripture in your head, verses that can be quoted from memory as the need arises. What is in your head does not necessarily impact what is in your heart. What is the point of quoting the Bible from memory if you do not remember to apply its teachings to your own life?

Remember the Stories

Preachers need to take time to be immersed in the lessons, stories, and characters found in the Bible. We need to remember the encounter between Jesus and Satan in Matthew 4, where Jesus was able to answer every temptation set before him by Satan by answering with a quotation from Scripture that was obviously hidden in his heart. We need to remember the story in Acts 7 of Stephen, who was able to recall from memory the entire biblical story while he was preaching in Jerusalem, and who was able to answer his critics out of a deep familiarity with the Scriptures. God's Word was hidden in, or written upon, his heart.

Whether we read through the Bible in a systematic way (Genesis to Revelation) or concentrate on a certain genre of biblical literature (prophecy or epistles or parables) or follow a lectionary or some other reading schedule, preachers need to read and study the Bible until we can say to God with honesty, "I have hidden your word in my heart so I will not sin against you." The time spent in the solitary study of Scripture will inevitably pay dividends because things you read and ponder while alone will come rushing to mind in the midst of a moment in ministry you cannot anticipate.

Practice the Disciplines

In addition to Bible study, preachers ought to be regularly engaged in a life of spiritual disciplines that keep the soul well fed and nurtured. These disciplines might involve periods of fasting accompanied by readings from devotional books, extended periods of time in prayer, a systematic reading of a certain portion or genre of the Bible, and listening to sermons on tape or reading them in various journals and publications. If one of the great preachers in our country comes within fifty miles of where you live, it would be a rewarding spiritual exercise to travel to that location and share in that preaching experience. Those of us who preach for a living typically do not realize how much we need to *hear* a sermon until we find ourselves sitting like empty pitchers before a full fountain, waiting and needing to be filled.

Make Yourself Accountable

Another valuable spiritual discipline that can result in increased spiritual development for preachers is participation in some network of clergy or laity that provides accountability with respect to how we are doing our job and spending our time. We may think we are being effective simply because we are staying busy. We may not realize that out of the sixty-six books of the Bible, we have selected our sermon texts from only twenty to twenty-five of those books over the last year. We may not know that our sermons are losing their depth or focusing too often on the same doctrinal or topical issues, to the exclusion of what Paul calls "the whole counsel of God" (Acts 20:27, KJV).

An accountability group might consist of a weekly meeting of clergy for study or fellowship. It can mean offering feedback opportunities after a sermon to those who want to talk with you about your message for the day. An accountability group may be one wise and brutally honest church member who, if invited to do so, will offer you what author Lora Ellen McKinney calls "the view from the pew," which is in fact the title of one of her books.

However, *none* of this will happen if you allow yourself to be rushed and harried from task to task, from place to place, and from day to day. That is exactly what was happening to the disciples in Mark 6 when Jesus stepped in and said, "Come apart by yourselves to a quiet place and get some rest."

Keys to an Effective Preaching Ministry

I pray that the sharing of your faith may become effective when you perceive all the good that we may do for Christ. —Philemon 1:6

It is to be hoped that the passion of every preacher is to be effective in every aspect of his or her preaching ministry. We want to communicate clearly the gospel that has been entrusted to us. We want to articulate completely the truth of Christ and his salvation. We want to persuade powerfully the priorities of justice, mercy, and walking humbly with our God. The question is, How do we do it? I suggest that there are two fundamental keys to achieving a biblical level of excellence in our preaching.

1. Text and Topic Selection

Perhaps the most immediate challenges facing every preacher on a weekly basis is the matter of text and topic selection. "What to preach *next* Sunday?" is a question that begins to hang over the head of the preacher as soon as *this* Sunday's sermon has been delivered. This question (and the way we as preachers go about answering it) is the first key to an effective preaching ministry from week to week. What methodology will allow for the greatest integration of variety and creativity over a long period of time?

Some preachers approach their weekly text and topic selection through a process of random selection. They are led by thoughts that come to mind, by reading they have done, or by some comment they overheard, any of which may generate a sermon idea. There is no necessary connection to what was preached the previous Sunday, and no thought is given to how this sermon will lay a foundation for what might be preached in the weeks ahead. When you use random selection as your primary method for text and topic selection, every sermon stands alone, and each week finds the preacher scrambling to answer the question, "What can I preach about next Sunday?"

While the random selection of texts may be effective for some, let me, in the words of Paul, "show you a still more excellent way" (1 Corinthians 12:31). Preachers can commit themselves to one or more of four systems that can quickly inform them on what they might preach from week to week. A preacher may choose to use just one of them or shift from one to the other as the occasion presents itself. The four systems to be considered are as follows:

1. Preaching from the lectionary
2. Preaching from the liturgical calendar
3. Preaching from the national calendar
4. Preaching from theological themes

Each of these systems serves two basic functions. First, each allows for *more efficient preparation* by enabling the preacher to determine text and topic more quickly. Second, each makes for *more effective preaching* by pushing the preacher to engage a wider range of biblical and theological materials than might otherwise be the case. To put it another way, they prevent preachers from focusing on a narrow list of biblical books and theological issues or topics that stretch no further than the preacher's own interests or experiences.

Preaching from the Lectionary

The lectionary is a three-year cycle of texts that leads the preacher through all the books of the Bible and through all the major seasons and themes of the Christian calendar. The lectionary pushes the preacher to choose texts not only from 1 and 2 Corinthians, but also from 1 and 2 Chronicles; not only from Romans, but also from Ruth and Revelation. The lectionary is a reminder that the Bible contains sixty-six books, all of which are canonical, authoritative, and deserving of being included in our preaching schedule. Preaching from all the books of the Bible is made easier by the lectionary, because each week the preacher is given four texts to consider. There is always a psalm as well as a second Old Testament passage drawn from the Law, History, Prophets, or Wisdom books. There will also be two texts taken from the New Testament: one from one of the Gospels and from one of the Epistles. If the lectionary is followed on a regular basis, a preacher will undoubtedly end up considering material that might never have arisen if text and topic selection were based on random selection.

At the same time, the lectionary challenges the preacher to consider the theology and proclamation possibilities of the major holy days and seasons in the Christian calendar. Among these are Advent, Christmas, Epiphany, Palm Sunday, Lent, Maundy Thursday, Good Friday, Easter, and Pentecost. Many of these liturgical seasons stretch out for many Sundays, thus providing extensive sermon material.

Following the lectionary provides a natural link between the messages to be preached from one Sunday to the next. A preaching series (which we will examine more closely in Section VI) is a good way to approach text and topic selection, and using the lectionary facilitates the development of such a series.

The lectionary approach to text and topic selection will inevitably offer some theological and topical issues that lie outside the preacher's comfort zone of knowledge or present understanding. That is no excuse to skip the suggested text and search for some easier or more familiar material. The issue of text and topic selection should challenge the preacher to greater study and to a broader understanding of biblical materials. The Revised Standard Version translates Paul's words in Acts 20:27, "I did not shrink from declaring to you the whole counsel of God." Indeed, declaring the whole counsel of God should be our goal as preachers. This goal is greatly aided when we have a system that moves us beyond the verses we already know and beyond the material with which we are familiar and comfortable.

Preaching from the Liturgical Calendar

For those who do not want to limit themselves to the scheduled texts found in the lectionary, there is still much to be gained by remaining aware of the liturgical season in considering "What to preach next Sunday?" **Advent** is a four-week season that usually begins on the Sunday after Thanksgiving and takes us to the Sunday before Christmas. This is a great time to preach about such varied themes and topics as waiting on the Lord, the second coming of Christ, and Jesus as the fulfillment of Old Testament prophecy, as well as on the texts that deal with the birth and ministry of John the

Baptist, who was preparing the way for the coming of the Messiah.

Christmas opens the door to speaking about the incarnation of Jesus Christ and the wonderful and mysterious notion of "God with us" that is captured in the word *Emmanuel*. One can also deal with the power and possibilities of the virgin birth or with the fact that news of Christ's birth was first shared with the poor shepherds who lived marginalized lives in Jewish society.

John 3:16 is a great Christmas text because it focuses entirely on the purpose of the birth of Jesus: that the world through him might be saved. Preachers might also consider exploring the fact that Paul makes only one reference to the birth of Jesus Christ, and this occurs in the rather abrupt statement in Galatians 4:4. Despite the prominence of the Christmas holiday in most churches, it should not be lost on us that Paul's emphasis was on the resurrection, without which we as preachers would have nothing worthwhile to say.

The next season in the liturgical cycle is **Epiphany**, which commences two weeks after Christmas Day and marks the appearance of the magi from the East in the birth story of Matthew 2. While Jesus was born into a Jewish culture and circumcised under Jewish law, Epiphany reminds us that his birth was for the sake of the whole world. The question is how an event that was meant to have an impact on the whole world could be made known when it occurred in such a remote location as Bethlehem in the Roman province of Judea. It was the wise men (magi) who symbolically carried the message of the birth of Jesus into the wider world. Thus, Epiphany provides an occasion for preaching on a variety of missions and evangelism themes.

Lent is a season in mid-winter that begins with Ash Wednesday and continues for forty days (not counting weekends). This is a time for self-examination, for focusing on spiritual disciplines such as fasting and self-sacrifice, and for breaking the power of the attitudes and addictions that prevent us from enjoying a closer relationship with God. Aristotle said, "The unexamined life is not worth living." Lent is that season of the church year when this aspect of Christian living can be addressed. "Search me, O God, and know my heart; test me and know my thoughts. See if there is any wicked way in me, and lead me in the way everlasting" (Psalm 139:23-24). That is what Lent is all about.

Next comes **Holy Week**, which runs from Palm Sunday through Easter. It includes observances that fall on Maundy Thursday, any traditions or events dealing with the Upper Room and Garden of Gethsemane, and finally commemoration of Good Friday. The preacher's focus is thus on the trials facing Jesus, as well as on the crucifixion. Topics such as the doctrine of substitutionary atonement, the meaning of the Lord's Supper, the resurrection of Jesus, the prospect of our own resurrection as a benefit of faith in Christ, and the role of Christ as the fulfillment of the Suffering Servant passages in Isaiah are all appropriate during this week and for several weeks thereafter.

The last of the major liturgical events, **Pentecost,** occurs fifty days (seven Sundays) after Easter. This is probably the most *under*celebrated day on the Christian calendar so far as most non-Pentecostal Christians are concerned. However, it ought to be regarded as equal in importance with the others. Pentecost celebrates the day when the Holy Spirit was breathed upon the disciples in Jerusalem (see Acts 2). Under the influence of the Holy Spirit, the early church moved beyond the Jerusalem community to locations throughout the entire Mediterranean world.

Pentecost should in no way be viewed as an event or doctrine that is limited to the issue of glossolalia (speaking in tongues). Pentecost suggests sermons on the doctrine of the Trinity, with emphasis on the work of the Holy Spirit, as well as on the topics of global evangelization and the multiethnic makeup of the church, as was the case with the crowd in Acts 2 at Peter's famous sermon. Pentecost is also a good time to preach about the doctrine of the church (ecclesiology), since its official origins are traced to this event.

Preaching from the National Calendar

A third system for text and topic selection is based on keeping track of the various secular holidays that are a part of the national calendar. **New Year's Day** is a great time for Philippians 3:13-14: "Beloved, I do not consider that I have made it my own; but this one thing I do: forgetting what lies behind and straining forward to what lies ahead, I press on toward the goal for the prize of the heavenly call of God in Christ Jesus." **Martin Luther King Jr. Day** is a good time for preaching from some of the prophetic texts such as Micah 6:8 and Amos 5:21-24. It is also a good time to preach about creating "the beloved community," a society where prejudice, bigotry, and racial divisions have been eliminated.

Valentine's Day may be overlooked as a sentimental event useful only for flower and candy sales unless you determine to appropriate it for a discussion of the difference between the *eros* love between people and the *agape* love of God. First Corinthians 13 and 1 John 4:7-21, as well as the many references to God's "loving-kindness" are appropriate on the Sunday nearest Valentine's Day. **Memorial Day** is, of course, a time to remember those who fought and died in our nation's wars. However, it is also a time when issues of death and grief and our hope for life after death can be addressed.

Independence Day should bring to mind such passages as: "For freedom Christ has set us free. Stand firm, therefore, and do not submit again to a yoke of slavery" (Galatians 5:1). You might also use: "So if the Son makes you free, you will be free indeed" (John 8:36). In a country governed by elected officials, the preacher can remind us of the last words of David, who urged Solomon to govern the nation with righteousness and in the fear of God (2 Samuel 23:3-4). In our ongoing struggle over the separation of church and state, the preacher might also consider the implication of the verse that proclaims, "Happy is the nation whose God is the LORD" (Psalm 33:12). In short, the Fourth of July in America is an occasion for more than just fireworks and cookouts; it is an opportunity for some important preaching.

Labor Day is the next major holiday on the national calendar. At a time when jobs are being outsourced from the United States and when prevailing wage and minimum-wage issues are being debated, this is a good time for such themes as "the worker is worth his keep" (Matthew 10:10, NIV) or "you shall not muzzle an ox while it is treading out the grain" (1 Corinthians 9:9; cf. Deuteronomy 25:4). It is also a good time to encourage people to embrace work over welfare, as suggested in the words, "Anyone unwilling to work should not eat" (2 Thessalonians 3:10).

Columbus Day reminds us of the legitimate concerns of Native Americans whose ancestral homelands have been lost, whose tribal groups are still used as mascots for sports teams, and whose history remains distorted by Hollywood films. It is also a time to talk about ethnic diversity in society in general and in the church in particular. Finally, this is a good time to remind ourselves of America's place in a world that includes Europe, the Caribbean, and all the other continents and cultures, as just another member in our global community.

November provides us with two special observances: **Veterans Day** and **Thanksgiving Day**. The first allows us a chance not only to honor those who have served in the armed forces, but to consider the full range of issues that touch upon war and peace in this age of nuclear, biological, and chemical weapons. Both Isaiah 2:4 and Micah 4:3 challenge us to work for the day when nations will "study war no more." Jesus reminded us in the Garden of Gethsemane, "All who take the sword will perish by the sword" (Matthew 26:52). This is also a time to consider the bloody conflicts found in Joshua and Judges in the stories of the conquest of the Holy Land. The Old Testament refers to God as the Holy Warrior, but when is it ever right for nations to state, "God is on our side"?

Thanksgiving affords us an opportunity to preach on any number of psalms, including 95, 100, and

103–7. It is a good season to remind ourselves of the prosperity we enjoy as a nation in a world in which the vast majority of people live in unimaginable poverty. However, we should not limit our thanksgiving to matters of material resources and daily bread. We should also be thankful for the "bread of life" that continually nourishes our souls, as well as for the Living Bread that came down out of heaven (John 6:32-35).

Just as important is the story of the first Thanksgiving in North America when the Native Americans, who shared their food with strangers, kept alive the English settlers of the Plymouth colony in Massachusetts. This is a good basis for a sermon on being "my brother's keeper" (Genesis 4:9) or on the admonition "to share your bread with the hungry, and bring the homeless poor into your house" (Isaiah 58:7).

Preaching from Theological Themes

The fourth and final system for text and topic selection has nothing to do with dates or seasons of the national or liturgical calendar. Instead, it consists of a conscious attempt to preach according to a theological rotation that addresses key Christian doctrines in five areas: God, Jesus Christ, the Holy Spirit, the fallen nature of humanity, and the mission of the church in the world. It would be a rewarding exercise for a preacher to begin with a blank sheet of paper or a blank computer screen and then to list all the aspects of the doctrine of God that come to mind. Those aspects would doubtless include such designations as Creator, Sovereign, Judge, Redeemer, Provider, Shelter, Lawgiver, and Liberator. It would extend to such topics as the will of God, the grace of God, the love of God, the mercy of God, the laws or commandments of God, and the power of God.

A similar list could be compiled for each of the other four categories. The list for Christ could include such events as his birth, miracles, parables, passion, resurrection, and second coming, as well as his prayer life, attitudes toward those who were marginalized, and the seven "I am" sayings scattered throughout the Gospel of John. The list for the Holy Spirit could include the work of the Holy Spirit to empower and equip us for ministry, to comfort us in times of distress, and to be the active presence of the power of God in our lives and in our world.

The list on the fallen nature of humanity would take us into the problem of human sin in all its forms—a woefully underaddressed preaching topic in our power-of-positive-thinking society. This list would also allow us to talk about justification by faith and the vanity of works righteousness. The list for the mission of the church allows for any sermon that deals with denominational emphases, including particular doctrinal practices that involve baptism or Communion, issues of stewardship and tithing, evangelism and missions, ecumenical and interfaith relations, and matters of church and society.

There are a multitude of doctrines, beliefs, and practices that we as preachers should attempt to discuss in our sermons. Why do Christians take Communion or engage in baptism, and why does *our* particular congregation do those things in the way in which we do? What is the nature of Scripture in its relationship to the church? Is it infallible, inerrant, or just instructive and suggestive? Why are some churches self-governed and autonomous while others have bishops and a jurisdictional structure? Does belief in the active power of the Holy Spirit make one a Pentecostal, and why should persons who are not Pentecostal observe Pentecost Sunday? What is the meaning of ordination, and how does that relate to the idea of "the priesthood of all believers"?

Doctrinal preaching is an opportunity to clarify our approach to Christian faith and action. It is a chance to provide the biblical, theological, and even historical foundations for the ways in which we approach the Christian faith. No longer do we simply notice that other people seem to think and act differently than we do, but in doctrinal preaching we are attempting to help our congregation understand the reasons for those differences and for our own particular preferences and approaches.

One could preach a doctrinal sermon as a follow-up to a question that was raised in a Bible study, in a youth group meeting, by any member of the church, or by someone in the wider community who has come looking for clarification on a specific doctrinal issue. There is a caution to be issued at this point. When it comes to answering questions from individuals through the delivery of sermons to the whole congregation, the preacher should be careful to limit such sermons to issues that either have or should have broad interest in the congregation. Small, technical concerns, for example, about the use of grape juice versus real wine in Communion can and should be answered privately unless there is a wide concern within the church about the matter that has been brought to your attention.

The greatest challenge of doctrinal preaching is deciding which doctrines to address. There are many possibilities as one considers the content of Scripture, theology and ethics, and Christian and denominational history. The easiest way to proceed with narrowing the list is to draw the doctrines you plan to discuss from some widely honored and commonly agreed upon document that is affirmed by the church or your denomination. The Apostles' Creed comes to mind as one of the best places to look. There are also various confessions and covenants used by different denominations that point toward their core beliefs. Making use of these documents serves to keep you focused on the *major* doctrines and away from the obscure topics that may be of interest to you and one other person in the church.

Using one or more of these four systems should guarantee that you will never have a shortage of sermon texts and topics and that you will not waste time searching for an answer to the preacher's perennial "what to preach next week" question. With the lectionary, the liturgical seasons, the national calendar, and a regular rotation of five nearly limitless theological doctrines, the preaching pump should always be primed, and our planning and preaching schedules should always be fresh, creative, and relevant.

Keep in mind that the liturgical holy days and national holidays do not account for every Sunday of the year. Plenty of time remains for those random-selection sermons that may spark your interest even if they do not coincide with any noteworthy season on the calendar of the church or the nation. Moreover, no preacher should ignore those "breaking news" events such as the terrorist attacks on September 11, 2001, the tsunami of 2004, the hurricanes of 2005, or some other worldwide, national, or local catastrophe that necessitates the preacher's attempt to provide some biblical or theological perspective for the church. If a world leader is killed, if a major disaster takes place, if the home team wins the World Series, or if some controversial issue suddenly breaks into the news cycle (such as a vote for same-sex marriage, the ordination of gay clergy, a U.S. Supreme

Court ruling to expand or limit abortion law under *Roe v. Wade*), a preacher might be forgiven for postponing until next week a sermon on the third commandment or the fourth beatitude.

2. Goals and Outcomes

The second key to an effective preaching ministry is the understanding that every sermon needs to be received and then responded to in some way that the preacher may suggest and that the Spirit may direct. Good preaching is not all about *hearing* the message; it moves from hearing to *heeding,* or taking to heart what has just been heard. Keep in mind the message in the famous Jewish prayer (called the Shema) found in Deuteronomy 6:4. It says, "Hear, O Israel: The LORD is our God, the LORD alone." This verse and the prayer it supports are not entirely about the people hearing a message on the character of God or the notion of monotheism. The verse hinges on the word *shema,* which in Hebrew means both "to hear with the ear" and "to heed; to act upon what has just been heard."

Henry H. Mitchell has observed that every sermon ought to be preached with a behavioral outcome in mind. There ought to be something that the sermon is asking or urging the listeners to do after the message is finished and the worship service has ended. Your sermon is not ready to be preached until you have thought through what the outcome or the response ought to be as a result of what you are going to say. The responses may vary from week to week and from sermon to sermon, but what does not vary and what *should* not vary is the practice of designing your sermon in such a way that it becomes clear to listeners what you expect from them in terms of a behavioral response.

This step in the preaching process is one of the things that separates us as preachers from news reporters. A reporter talks about the "what"; nothing else is expected from a reporter except the truthful telling of the facts. This is "what" happened. Not so with the preacher, for our job is to move beyond the "what" to the far more significant issue of "so what?" So what if God is the author of creation? So what if the Bible is the revealed will of God? So what if Jesus died on the cross as atonement for my sin? What does any of that have to do with me? Preachers do not stop at reporting on the facts of the Bible; they call upon their listeners to make a faithful response to the facts and truths just communicated.

One of the most useful approaches addressing behavioral responses to sermons comes from Robert McCracken in his book *The Making of the Sermon*. He discusses four possible behavioral responses to a sermon: (1) kindle the mind, (2) energize the will, (3) disturb the conscience, and (4) stir the heart. Sometimes the response you want is to have people think or rethink an issue or a position on some subject. Other times you want to motivate them to move beyond thinking to taking some specific action on the matter at hand. Other times the objective of the sermon is to persuade people to change their sinful behavior, to repent of ungodly conduct, to renounce their unholy practice, and to "come to Jesus." (Remember that both Jesus and John the Baptist preached about repentance in their very first sermons.) Finally, there are the sermons in which the desired outcome is that people will be encouraged to carry on in the face of great hardship because they know "the Lord is with me."

Kindle the Mind

A sermon whose goal is to kindle the mind might encourage people to think about a complex or controversial topic on which many may still be undecided or divided. This might be done by helping the congregation understand how believers who are equally devout and faithful can be divided on a certain biblical teaching. One can also set forth the rivaling positions held by groups of Christians on issues such as abortion, same-sex marriage, the right to die, stem cell research, or the "justness" of a particular war. Rather than telling people what to believe, when we kindle the mind we provide people with the pertinent information and encourage them to think through the issue for themselves.

Kindling the mind also works when the goal is to encourage people to *re*think a point of view. A sermon might urge people to consider views they may have held since their childhood about women in ministry, race relations, the proper forms for Communion or baptism, how broadly or narrowly the congregation's benevolence ministries ought to extend, or whether to enter into ecumenical or interfaith dialogue. No immediate action is to be expected except that the person think about what has been said.

It is not necessary and it may not be useful for the preacher to weigh down this kind of sermon with his or her personal views on the issue. That might prejudice some listeners one way or the other and keep them from thinking through the issue for themselves. What is most important for a sermon attempting to kindle the mind is that the issue be both relevant and pertinent. This kind of sermon might help people come to grips with an issue about which people of faith are already talking. Or it could address a matter of Christian faith and doctrine that needs to be revisited.

Energize the Will

A time may come in the life of a church when a believer or a congregation needs to take action but the believer or people lack motivation. In this instance, the goal of the sermon is to energize the will. The time to think has passed; the time to act has come. Demosthenes and Cicero were two great orators of the classical Greek era in the third century B.C. It was said that after Cicero spoke, people would say, "What a fine speaker he is." However, when they heard Demosthenes, they said, "Let us go and fight against the king." One person informed, but the other inspired the hearers to action.

The Bible invites us to embrace any number of practices that we are slow to adopt, including tithing, growing multicultural congregations, doing ministry with and among disadvantaged communities, taking a stand against some injustice, and introducing some innovation into the worship service. At some point people need to be invited, encouraged, and challenged to act on the matter at hand. When Peter, James, and John first met Jesus, they had had a frustrating night of fishing; they hadn't caught a single fish. But after borrowing their boat to preach a sermon to an encroaching crowd, Jesus told them to cast their nets into deep water. Men who were fishermen by trade were initially reluctant to accept advice on fishing from a carpenter, but Jesus pressed his case and gave them the incentive, the motivation to act—and it paid off in more fish than their own nets and boat could handle (see Luke 5:1-11)!

Joshua challenged the people of Israel to "choose this day whom you will serve" (Joshua 24:14). Elijah challenged Israel, "How long will you go limping with two different opinions? If the LORD is God, follow him; but if Baal, then follow him" (1 Kings 18:21). Jesus challenged the rich young ruler: "Sell all that you own and distribute the money to the poor . . . then come, follow me" (Luke 18:22). Paul urged the Corinthian church by saying, "Be imitators of me, as I am of Christ" (1 Corinthians 11:1). Over and over in Revelation we encounter the phrase, "Let anyone who has an ear listen to what the Spirit is saying to the churches" (see Revelation 2:7). Each of these is a call to action; each is designed to energize the will of those who heard the message.

If the text calls for action, there must come a point in the sermon when the listeners are challenged to respond. If the preacher knows there is something preventing people from taking the step the text is demanding, that preacher needs to consider how to confront the obstacle, to encourage people to step over it and press on toward the required actions. People may or may not *take* the action that is desired; this is the lesson of Ezekiel in chapters 3 and 33, where the words of the watchman were heard but not heeded. What the preacher can and must do is to set forth the action that is required or requested and to attempt to motivate people to act.

Disturb the Conscience

There are occasions in preaching when the desired outcome of the sermon is to set before the people the related issues of sin, confession, repentance, and restoration. Romans 3:23 remains central to our preaching task: "All have sinned and fall short of the glory of God." The same can be said for Romans 7:18: "For I do not do the good I want, but the evil I do not want is what I do." One of the goals of preaching is to use these and other texts to lift before people the standard of Christian conduct and confession that the Bible challenges us to embrace and then to hold people accountable if and when they fall short of that goal. There are times when preaching must name the evils we confront and the "sin that so easily entangles" (Hebrews 12:1, NIV).

Sometimes attitudes and behaviors need to be abandoned and lifestyles need to be altered. Oppression and exploitation of people based on race, gender, age, or other factors must end. Sometimes the preacher's goal is to so concentrate on some sin that the sermon unsettles and disturbs the conscience of each person who may be engaged in such actions or who may hold the attitudes being challenged that day. Having disturbed the conscience, the preacher must move on to the next step by challenging those people to repent.

The God of the Bible is full of love and grace, but Scripture also establishes commandments to be obeyed, disciplines to be practiced, and justice to be pursued by the people of God. When God's people fall short of what God expects and of what the Bible clearly sets forth, God needs someone to speak whose words will disturb the conscience of those in the community of faith whose salt has lost its savor and whose light no longer shines (see Matthew 5:13-16). At the same time, preaching must reach out to those who do not now believe and who have never made a confession of faith in Christ by challenging them to abandon the lives they are living. People need to be urged to see that life without Christ is unfulfilling and insecure.

Stir the Heart

An effective preaching ministry will always recognize that every Sunday welcomes people in the congregation who need the gospel to help them through some storm that is raging in their lives and to remind them in the face of their trials and tribulations that "the Lord will make a way somehow." God is faithful. God's promises are secure. God's strength is more than sufficient in helping us bear our heaviest burdens. People are coping with cancer and other diseases, divorce, unemployment, troubled marriages, wayward children, depression and despair, midlife crises, and issues of low self-esteem. They need to know that God is not powerless in the face of their particular problems. There is a word from the Lord for their situation. And when that word is declared in their hearing, their response might range from "Hallelujah" to

"Thank you, Jesus," from "Lord, have mercy" to a hearty "Amen."

Whether you preach these texts because they appear in your text selection rotation or because you insert them in support of the point you are trying to make, people need to know that "the steadfast love of the LORD never ceases, his mercies never come to an end; they are new every morning; great is your faithfulness" (Lamentations 3:23). They need to know that "neither death, nor life, nor angels, nor rulers, nor things present, nor things to come, nor powers, nor height, nor depth, nor anything else in all creation, will be able to separate us from the love of God in Christ Jesus our Lord" (Romans 8:38-39).

Samuel Johnson said, "People do not so much need to be informed as to be reminded." People may already know about the power and love and compassion of God, but their situation at any given moment can be so overwhelming that they lose sight of the resources of their faith. Stirring the heart, in part, entails reminding people of what they already know: "The one who is in you is greater than the one who is in the world" (1 John 4:4).

3. Keeping Your Balance

The reason for discussing these four sermon outcomes and four systems for text and topic selection is to encourage preachers to strive for variety in their preaching from week to week—both in terms of the subject matter and of the behavioral response that is being called for. Rotate your themes and topics from week to week so that people come to the time of the sermon with a sense of anticipation about what might be coming next. Shift your desired outcomes from week to week as well. Sometimes you want thought and reflection, but at other times the desired goal might be action, repentance, or celebration.

Nothing is worse for a preacher than being so predictable that people are really no longer listening. In short, not only is variety the spice of life, but diversity in text and topic selection and variety in sermon goals and outcomes are also the keys to a successful, long-term preaching ministry.

Preaching Styles and Forms

Jesus Christ is the same yesterday and today and forever. —Hebrews 13:8

The voice of the Christian preacher has lost some of its authority in America today because the culture and conditions within which preaching now takes place are radically different from what they were just a generation ago, not to mention two millennia ago. Jesus Christ is the same yesterday, today, and forever, but the world in which his gospel is being preached has changed dramatically, not only since the first century when Jesus lived, but over the last fifty years since most Americans were born.

1. Preaching in a Postmodern Context

In the mid-1960s, folk singer Bob Dylan announced a shift in the views and values held by people in this country when he sang, "The times they are a'changing." That song may have been among the first indicators of the changes in American society that produced what is now referred to as *postmodernism*. This shift has had an impact on every aspect of our culture, including the role and place of religion. Preachers cannot afford to ignore the implications of this shift in our culture, because it has the potential to determine how people will receive information, including religious information delivered through sermons.

From the church's perspective, postmodernism speaks to a time when the authority of leaders (preachers included), popular confidence in institutions (the church included), and widespread familiarity with religious literature (the Bible included) can no longer be assumed. Preaching entails asking people to listen to a message with which they are increasingly unfamiliar from a person whom they may no longer revere. Furthermore, this preaching task takes place within the walls of an institution that many increasingly distrust. "The times they are a'changing." Indeed, they have already changed.

Postmodern society is also a place where the presumed identification of the United States of America as "a Christian nation" is no longer embraced. America has evolved into a secular culture with a First Amendment to the Constitution that guarantees the rights of all religions to function in our society, as well as the right not to be religious at all. The sight of Muslim mosques and minarets is becoming common in urban centers and suburban areas of the country.

Scientology, frequently discussed on radio and television, has high-profile advocates, such as the actor Tom Cruise, who has defended his religious tradition on the nationally syndicated *Oprah Winfrey Show*.

As preachers, we believe that Jesus Christ is the same, but the challenge of today's gospel ministry is to communicate Christ's unchanging truths to a population that has changed dramatically in the last generation. How do we establish our own authority, the church's integrity, and the Bible's value as a guidebook for life in a culture that questions the legitimacy of all three?

Ethical Issues and America's Religious Discussions

There is quite literally an epic struggle under way about the place of religion in postmodern society. It is centered on such issues as the origins of the universe and involves such debates as evolution versus creationism and the more recent "intelligent design" theory. In addition, state after state is turning to the ballot box to determine whether the nature of the marriage union will remain one man and one woman. The question is whether our preaching is addressing the questions our people are asking and over which they may be agonizing.

Unlike any previous generation of Americans, those who were born within the last thirty years have been born into a society wherein any reference to preachers might just as easily generate thoughts of sexual or

financial scandals as it does thoughts of someone who
is faithfully handling the Word of God. Any reference
to the church might set off alarm bells about religious
intolerance in a multicultural society or a passionate
preoccupation with divisive social issues such as abortion and homosexuality. Unlike most of their parents
and grandparents, the majority of postmodern
Americans have not been raised on a diet of Sunday
school, Vacation Bible School, church-sponsored sum-
mer camps, and churches with active youth ministry
programs. As a result, young adults today may be
largely unfamiliar with the stories, characters, doctrines, and even vocabulary of the Bible.

Preaching and High-Tech Communication

Anyone who is attempting to preach the gospel in this
postmodern world must understand how the audience
has changed over the last two or three decades. People
have shifted from the nightly news broadcasts on TV
to the around-the-clock news available on the
Internet. They have become less dependent on land-
based telephones, preferring instead to rely on their
cell phones (which may be built into their PDAs—
Personal Data Assistants) and IMing (Instant
Messaging) on the computer. Twenty-first century
people have become accustomed to multimedia presentations of sights and sounds and information

projected on a screen. They make use of the latest audio technology and streaming of information on handheld devices they carry with them all the time. Today's preacher is challenged to consider what it takes to get people who live in the postmodern world to slow down and listen to a person talk to them about a religious theme for twenty or thirty minutes.

Preaching and the Local Church

There is another factor that cannot be overlooked by those who seek to preach the gospel in the twenty-first century: cable television ministries. While it is true that many in the new generation are unchurched there are many others who are inundated with exposure to some of the greatest preachers in the country every night in the comfort of their own homes. This exposure may be the positive motivation that comes from Joel Osteen of the 40,000-member Lakewood Church in Houston, Texas; the Bible teaching that comes from John Hagee of Cornerstone Baptist Church in San Antonio, Texas; the trademark high energy and passion of Bishop G. E. Patterson of the Church of God in Christ; or the magnetic appeal of T. D. Jakes, who seems to be on some cable TV station almost every night. Those who come to hear preaching in local churches have been listening to good, and sometimes even great, preaching throughout the week. How does a pastor in the local church compete with these media-driven, multimillion-dollar funded, megachurch pastors?

The local pastor does not define what preaching is as a form, nor does the local pastor set the standard for the skill level at which it can be performed. That work is done every night on national cable television networks by Paula White and Joyce Meyer, as well as by D. James Kennedy and Charles Stanley. It is also done all day long by radio preachers ranging from David Jeremiah to Tony Evans to Chuck Swindoll. People have read about the 50,000 members at Saddleback Church in California, and many of them have read Rick Warren's book *The Purpose-Driven Life*.

In other words, many of the people who show up at church on Sunday are not empty pitchers coming to a fountain waiting to be filled. Instead, they are steady consumers of religious information that comes at them nonstop from radio, TV, church-sponsored conferences, direct-mail literature, and Internet sources. When they sit down to hear our sermons, they are not likely to be impressed with twenty-five minutes of monotone dialogue on some obscure aspect of denominational dogma or doctrine. This is made all the worse when the preacher decides to read the sermon from a manuscript with his or her eyes glued to the pages on the lectern as opposed to surveying the people in the congregation.

It is difficult to imagine anything that is harder to

sustain in the rushed, high-tech, soundbyte culture that is twenty-first-century America than the practice of preaching. This raises the question of how preachers should approach their work so they can communicate effectively with people who are being shaped every day by postmodern society. How do you plan and present sermons to people who are constantly exposed to news, information, entertainment, instant communication, and world-class speakers and workshop leaders? How does one preach to people who have a greater awareness of the presence and claims of non-Christian religious traditions than ever before in American history? The answer is to concentrate on mastering the forms and styles of preaching in order to be able to share the gospel with a diverse audience through the use of diverse aspects of communication.

2. Preaching Forms and Types

Preaching cannot be defined by referring to a single form of sermon structure and delivery. It can be done in a wide variety of forms, forms that may shift from week to week. The list of forms or sermon types includes expository, topical, narrative (storytelling), and extemporaneous. This list of sermon types must be considered partly in relation to the various occasions when a sermon is likely to be called for or expected by the congregation. These occasions include Sunday morning worship services, evangelistic revivals, funeral eulogies, wedding homilies, college and university chapel services, ecumenical and interfaith dialogues, prison ministry events, seasonal events such as a Good Friday or Lenten service, and special programs geared toward youth or adults and for men or women.

It is well-known that if a major league baseball player steps into the batter's box against a pitcher who can throw only one pitch, the advantage automatically goes to the hitter because there is no question about what pitch is about to be thrown. It does not matter how fast the pitcher's fastball is, and it does not matter how much movement is on the curve ball. A major league hitter will more than likely get a hit if he knows that the pitcher can throw only one type of pitch. For this reason the best major league pitchers today have achieved mastery over three or four pitches, choosing among the fast ball, slider, curve ball, fork ball, and changeup.

Not only do those pitchers know how to throw a variety of pitches, but they also have developed the ability to throw them from multiple angles: overhand (from above the shoulder), side-arm (with the ball kept at waist level), or with a few, underhanded, where the pitch is released at knee level. All of this is done to prevent the batter from knowing what pitch is coming next or from what angle the ball will be approaching. It forces the batter to devote full attention to what the pitcher is going to do next.

Preachers can learn many things from pitchers, not the least of which is the importance of mastering a variety of forms and the ability to deliver them in a variety of ways based on the circumstances. This mastery of form and style can go a long way toward getting and holding the attention of a postmodern congregation. If people think they already know what you are going to say—or if you say it in a way that is boring and uninspired—their minds will quickly drift to whatever they have planned to do as soon as the service ends. If, however, there is an expectation that something new will be said, and that the message will be appropriate for the setting and relevant to the issues of the day, there is a greater likelihood that people will come out to church with the words of Jeremiah 37:17 in their hearts and on their lips: "Is there any word from the Lord?"

Of course, that Scripture is not only about the question raised by Zedekiah: "Is there any word from the Lord?" It is also about the answer given by Jeremiah: "Yes, there is!" It is the right of the people to raise the question of Zedekiah, and it is the responsibility of the preacher to give the answer of Jeremiah. We need to be sure that we are bringing a word from the Lord when we stand to preach, and we need to be sure we are designing and delivering that word in ways that help to assure that people will both hear and heed what is being said.

How do you preach so the people who enter the church from different backgrounds can all leave the church saying, "I was glad when they said to me, 'Let us go to the house of the LORD!'" (Psalm 122:1)? The solution is to be intentional about the forms and styles of preaching that are available to you and to vary your use of those tools from week to week.

Expository Preaching

The phrase that is perhaps most commonly associated with preaching comes from the ministry of Billy Graham, who while holding a Bible up in the air repeatedly proclaimed, "The Bible says!" That lingering image on the American consciousness has shaped what millions of people understand to be the essential form and function of preaching. Expository preaching focuses on some aspect of the content of Scripture. The goal of such a sermon is to gain some insight into the precise meaning of the text under consideration, and only secondarily to offer some suggestions about the implications of that text in the lives of those who hear the sermon.

As the word *expository* suggests, the goal is to set forth or "expose" the lessons contained within a given passage of Scripture. In expository preaching, every word is analyzed and every person—whether a major or minor character—is considered. One verse is studied in relationship to the verses that come before and after. The original languages are consulted to provide deeper insight into the precise meaning of the passage. Careful exegesis of the biblical text is essential, because it is the information learned in this solitary exercise that the preacher will later share with the congregation.

Given that a reduced level of familiarity with biblical material is a hallmark of the postmodern world, preachers would do well to develop some facility with this form of preaching. Many people may be interested simply to know what the Bible says, especially as it relates to the character of Christ or the existence and nature of God. People may be curious about the relationship between the nation of Israel and the surrounding people, such as the Philistines, the Phoenicians, and all the many "-ites" (Canaanites, Jebusites, Hittites, Hivites, Amorites, and more).

Expository preaching is a good place to do some work with the Hebrew and Greek texts, which offer insights into the original meaning of a passage. Expository preaching further requires some knowledge of the geography and topography of ancient Israel, as well as of the other nations that touch on the biblical story. In fact, one of the keys to effective expository preaching is a keen awareness of the geography of the Holy Land. What were the dimensions of the walled city of Jericho that fell before Joshua and the people of Israel? How far did Mary and Joseph have to travel and over what kind of territory when they went from Nazareth to Bethlehem as part of the Nativity story? Where is Samaria, and why might a Samaritan have been on the road described in the parable of the good Samaritan? What was the terrain of the path of the exodus from Egypt to Mt. Sinai, and how could that large a number of people have existed in so bleak an environment?

Just as important is an awareness of the other nations and their leaders that appear throughout the Scriptures. The biblical story is not limited to events that occurred within the limits of the land of Israel. The people of God go down into Egypt, over into Babylon, on to locations throughout Asia Minor, and into Greece and Rome, and finally they are sent by God unto the ends of the earth. The Bible speaks of pharaohs in Egypt; kings in Assyria, Babylon, and Greece; emperors in Persia; and Caesars in Rome. Who were these people, and what was the scope and reach of their power? Where were they located in proximity to Israel, and how did their paths intersect with the work that God was doing in history?

Expository preaching is meant to increase people's familiarity with the content, context, characters, and sociopolitical conditions present within whatever text is being considered. This kind of preaching works well in a sermon series in which you can work your way through some section of material over an extended period of time. A series on the Ten Commandments, the judges of Israel, the conquest of the Holy Land, the people gathered for Peter's sermon on the day of Pentecost, or the imprisonment stories of Peter and John in Jerusalem, of Paul in Philippi, or of John when he was exiled on the island of Patmos would all be excellent candidates for expository preaching topics. Other candidates include some of the oracles of the prophets, the Beatitudes of Jesus, key chapters in the Epistles such as 1 Corinthians 13 and Romans 8; and passages such as Psalm 23, the Lord's Prayer, the priestly blessing of Aaron in Numbers 6:22-25, and any of the benedictions found at the end of Paul's epistles. All these portions of biblical material lend themselves to expository preaching.

Finally, expository preaching is meant to re-create the world of the Bible so that the lessons learned by the characters in the text can be addressed and applied to the lives of the people who are hearing the sermon. For example, "Just as God brought down the walls for Joshua, God can bring down the strongholds that stand in our path today." "The same God who created the world out of nothing and brought forth life from the barren wombs of Sarah, Rebekah, Rachel, Hannah, and Elizabeth is able to bring forth miraculous outcomes in the world we live in today." "Just as God raised Lazarus and the daughter of Jairus and his own son, Jesus, from the dead, so too will God raise from the dead those who place their faith in God's Word and promises."

Expository preaching ought to be our primary approach to preaching, because it is the best way to impart the biblical knowledge that is so sadly lacking and so badly needed in the church today. However, there are other approaches to preaching that can also be used as long as the primary goal of imparting Bible knowledge is not forgotten.

Topical Preaching

There are times when you will be drawn to a topic or a theme on which you want to preach even before you have found a biblical text that sheds any light on that issue. You may feel the need to address some issue of peace or justice in the world; you may want to call people's attention to some aspect of human behavior or group dynamics. These topics might come from your daily readings, some report heard in the news media, a comment overheard in the airport, or questions resulting from your own observations of the world around you.

There are also topics that are already a point of much discussion within the church community. Stem cell research, abortion, capital punishment, creationism versus evolution versus intelligent design, the ordination of women, the nature of marriage, homogeneity as a principle of church growth, the applicability of the "just war" theory, and the appropriate role of patriotism in the life of the church are all topics that are under discussion in churches and parachurch groups across the country. There may be many opinions on those topics, but there may not have been any sermons offered to bring those topics under closer biblical scrutiny, thus leaving the news commentators and public opinion pollsters to have the last word. Topical preaching has an important role because it provides the occasion to interject God's Word and the church's teachings into the ongoing debates within our society. In a postmodern world, people may not stop to ask what the Bible says or what God may think about a certain issue or situation. A biblically based topical sermon can go a long way toward answering those questions.

Preaching on topics that are relevant and important is crucial if you are to have an effective, long-term preaching ministry. There are a great many topics that ought to be brought to the attention of the believing community. However, the goal of topical preaching is not dispensing information. Rather, the goal is and should always be illumination and understanding of how and why that topic is of importance to us as Christians. The goal is also to present what the Bible has to say on that topic, whether it is supportive of, neutral on, or in sharp opposition to what people in the church may already believe.

This kind of preaching, while common in churches across the country, is inherently risky because it often results in attempts to make a text say whatever we need it to say to fit the talk for the day.

Three-Point Dialectic Preaching

Many preachers automatically think about preaching in relationship to having "three points." Whether or not such points actually appear in the biblical passage, it is not unusual for a preacher to feel the need to find "three things" to say about the text in question. The three-point dialectic method may be employed in the context of other types of sermons, such as expository and topical. However, it deserves its own category because this method can serve as the essential approach to a sermon.

It might be useful to remember that the origin of the three-point sermon is rooted in the so-called dialectic method of Greek rhetoric and in the philosophy of George Hegel. (The best treatment of this approach to preaching is found in the book *The Certain Sound of the Trumpet* by Samuel DeWitt Proctor, Judson Press, 1994.)

A classical three-point sermon begins with a *thesis*, a statement of how things are or how things should be. A thesis may also be a truth that should be embraced or an action that should be taken. The *antithesis* is the obstacle or problem preventing the thesis from being achieved, whether the desired outcome is an action or an affirmation. The *synthesis* is the solution that the sermon is offering to the problem, or the setting forth of the ways in which the thesis can be accomplished. What makes this approach to preaching authentic is that the synthesis is the point at which the topic in question comes under biblical scrutiny and analysis.

It is important that the topic of this kind of sermon be one of current interest and importance within society. The Scripture text then serves as the lens through which that topic is considered. This approach can work with an endless list of topics and texts. However, three things are required from the preacher. First, the thesis statement or the topical concern must be faithfully stated and described. Second, the opposing point of view (or the reason why some people are not willing to act) must be considered with equal care. Finally, an honest and thorough exegetical review must take place as part of the synthesis.

Narrative Preaching and Biblical Storytelling

This approach to preaching focuses on recounting the sequence of events leading up to, including, and coming in the wake of a particular moment in time—the crossing of the sea, the first glimpse of the Promised Land, the act and agony of crucifixion, Paul's persecution of the church, and the effects on those present when a woman with an alabaster box anointed the feet of Jesus in the house of a Pharisee. These and dozens more are stories to be told, and the appeal is less to the brain and the notion of understanding and more to the senses and the creation of an experience. However, the desired outcome is the same: to draw listeners in by induction until they encounter the truth or lesson that the story seeks to communicate.

The key to biblical storytelling and narrative preaching is your own intimate familiarity with the biblical stories themselves. Preachers should work to develop a comfortable, storytelling familiarity with such Old Testament stories as the Creation, the Abraham-Isaac-Jacob narrative, the Exodus, the wandering in the wilderness, the conquest of the Promised Land, the monarchy from Saul to Solomon and the succession narratives that follow in 1 and 2 Kings, and the exile story from 722 B.C. to the return to Jerusalem in the Persian era. Stories also abound in the New Testament, including the passion of Christ, the work of the Holy Spirit in the spread of the church, the missionary journeys of Paul, the letters to the seven churches of Asia Minor, and the various apocalyptic and eschatological stories that speak about the end times.

Storytelling is an art form that preachers would do well to cultivate in their preaching. This is accomplished in part through the use of maximum detail so that the senses as well as the brain are all working to receive the message. Describe the heat of the sun; imagine the sound of the wind. Dramatize the pain someone was enduring. Depict the full palette of colors. Explore the sounds and scents. Utter dramatically, for emphasis, any words spoken as part of a conversation.

Biographical and Autobiographical Preaching

Preachers might choose to tell a story by focusing on their own or some other person's experience. In this regard, biographical and autobiographical preaching might be considered subcategories of narrative preaching.

The life of Jesus as recorded in the Bible is properly called "the greatest story ever told." The Nativity narrative is the beginning of this greatest story. In fact, the Bible is a compilation of fascinating and informative stories. A wonderful way to make the Bible come alive, especially for people who are more open to drama and presentation than they are to lecture or rhetoric, is to become adept at presenting these stories in the context of preaching. Think about making use of first- or third-person character development. Third-person preaching corresponds with a biography wherein an objective observer narrates or recounts the events in the life of a certain person (e.g., "Noah worked feverishly to finish the ark as the first drops of rain began to fall"). First-person preaching corresponds with autobiographical preaching, according to which the preacher speaks from the perspective of the character himself or herself (e.g., "The people who laughed at me while I was building a boat in the middle of the desert were now pleading with me to let them onboard as the flood waters rose around them").

People may enjoy hearing the story of Daniel in the lions' den or Paul and Silas in the Philippian jail less as a text to be analyzed and more as a story to be told from the point of view of one of the characters in the text. Telling the story of Moses from his personal exodus from Egypt after he killed an overseer to his leadership of the national exodus of the people of Israel from 430 years of slavery in Egypt could be done from a first- or third-person perspective. The same could be said about Ruth, Esther, and Job, not to mention Abraham as he led Isaac up Mt. Moriah, Namaan after he followed the advice of Elisha and washed himself in the Jordan River, the lepers after they had been healed by Jesus, or Peter in the hours after he had denied Jesus.

First- and third-person preaching, while they may be entertaining, are not designed primarily for entertainment purposes. They are meant to be inductive, to lead people deeper and deeper into a biblical scene or into a moment in the life of a biblical character when some significant encounter with God takes place. It should be noted that first- and third-person preaching do not have to be limited to the lead characters in a biblical text, such as Moses, Jesus, Paul, Mary, and Hannah. Often, there is something important to be learned when the story is viewed from the perspective of a minor character or even an antagonistic or villainous character, such as Pharaoh, Ahab, Jezebel, Herod, or Pontius Pilate.

The most important ingredient in this kind of preaching is detail with regard to the sights, sounds, emotions, and interactions of the character being discussed. How does the person look? What might he or she be wearing? What is the geography and topography that surrounds them? In my book *Living Water for Thirsty Souls*, I talk about being epigrammatical, communicating a message through sharply defined, richly detailed images. Create in the minds of the listeners the sunrise that was coming over the hills of Judea. Imagine the fear that gripped the shepherds when they were suddenly aroused by the glorious sight and sound of angels. What thoughts might have passed through the mind of the woman facing stoning after she was caught in the act of adultery? What might have been the reaction on Calvary when a Roman centurion declared concerning Jesus, "This was the son of God"?

The best way to learn how to tell stories is to get into the habit of *reading* stories. Preachers should read biographies and autobiographies, not merely for their information value, but also as object lessons on how to develop characters and narrate events. Television programs that offer biographies of historical characters are also useful for this purpose. The preacher who has told stories to children will remember that the richer and more graphic the sensory details, the more the child was drawn into the story. The sound of a twig snapping or an owl hooting, the smell of fresh morning air or a rotting carcass, the feel of wind and water blowing on your face as you sail across the Sea of Galilee as a sudden storm sweeps over the region—these are the kinds of details you need for this kind of preaching to be effective.

Projection screen images and bulletin covers can be useful tools with this form of preaching because they can help provide a basic context in which the character or story is set. You can ask people to refer to these aids as the sermon unfolds. Some preachers may want to take first-person preaching even further and employ costumes or props in order to increase the transformation from a traditional preaching style to character development.

Extemporaneous Speaking

Many believe that a preacher who does not make use of a manuscript in the delivering of the sermon is speaking extemporaneously. That may not be the case. As suggested earlier in this book, many preachers prepare complete manuscripts or detailed outlines but do not make use of them in the course of delivering the sermon. They speak without notes, but since they have done thorough preparation for a particular sermon or address, they cannot be said to be speaking extemporaneously.

Extemporaneous preaching may be understood in two ways. First, it describes a person who speaks on a topic without any prior study or preparation for that particular speaking event. The word *improvised* might be aptly applied in this instance. The speaker is working things out on the spot and with no earlier reflection on the subject done with that speech or sermon in mind. According to the second understanding of extemporaneous preaching, the speaker has given the subject matter to be discussed some prior thought, but not to the point of preparing a text or memorizing anything that is going to be said.

People often observe someone who "thinks well on his or her feet." This is a good attribute to have or to cultivate as a preacher, because there will inevitably be times when we are called upon to speak without prior warning, much less time for preparation. It is not uncommon for a preacher who visits a church during his or her vacation to be recognized and called upon to deliver the message that day. A preacher attending a funeral or memorial service may be called upon to bring words of condolence to the family. Even in your own church you may have a guest preacher scheduled whose flight is delayed or whose schedule changes at the last minute. With little or no warning, you must now stand in and say a word for the Lord. Take seriously the warning in 1 Peter 3:15: "Always be ready to make your defense to anyone who demands from you an accounting for the hope that is in you." As discussed in Section I, similarly embrace the exhortation of Paul to his protégé Timothy in 2 Timothy 4:2: "Be ready in season and out of season" (NKJV). Not all of your sermons will be delivered after weeks of prior notice and hours of prior preparation. This is a fact of life for many preachers.

There are ways to make the experience less traumatic. I keep in my wallet a list of twenty-five to thirty Scripture texts and sermon titles that I have preached before and could call to mind with little or no warning. It is a simple matter of reaching into my wallet and trying to match the sermon with the setting. You might also on a regular basis remind yourself of the stories in the Bible you know best, the sermon styles with which you are most comfortable, the simple sermon outcomes you would like to achieve, and any experiences in your own life that might allow you a point of entry into the discussion at hand or the text before you.

However, nothing is better preparation for extemporaneous preaching (which cannot be predicted) than regular reading and reflection on the Scriptures. Filling our hearts and minds with the Word of God will pay dividends when we open our mouths to preach with little or no preparation. Having said that, I must stress that extemporaneous preaching should not become the norm for our pulpit work. We should not wait until Sunday morning and then expect God to give us something to say. Every preacher needs to be held to the high standard of 2 Timothy 2:15: "Do your best to present yourself to God as one approved by him, a worker who has no need to be ashamed, rightly explaining the word of truth."

Sermon Design and Delivery

If the trumpet does not sound a clear call, who will get ready for battle?

—1 Corinthians 14:8, NIV

Paul offered a warning that every preacher should take seriously: "If the trumpet does not sound a clear call, who will get ready for battle?" This text joins together the two essential components of effective preaching: (1) a clear presentation of a biblical message with (2) the capacity to equip those who hear that message to live and work and witness more effectively.

The metaphor of the text is a military camp where the forces huddle inside the encampment in a relaxed mood, knowing that sentries are posted on the perimeters of the camp keeping watch for any approaching dangers. Those inside the camp know that when they hear the sound of the trumpet, they have to get ready for battle immediately because danger is upon them. However, if the trumpet does not blow loud and clear, or if the trumpet does not sound the appropriate tune that signals what action should be taken, those in the camp will be at risk of being killed or captured. Everything depends on the trumpet "sounding a clear call."

As preachers we need to view our work with an equal sense of urgency and importance; we need to be sure that our sermons sound a clear call. We need to be sure that those who hear our sermons hear an authentic word from God and understand exactly what actions they should take in response to what they have heard. Our chances of sounding a clear call are greatly increased when we craft our sermons according to reliable principles that govern sermon design and delivery.

1. Sermon Preparation

In a recent Professional Golfers' Association tournament, Tiger Woods and John Daley, two of the best golfers on the pro tour, found themselves going into a one-hole playoff for the championship. A sportswriter who was covering the event reported that, in preparation for teeing off to begin the playoff, Tiger Woods took several practice swings with his driver while John Daley took in several puffs of a cigarette. Each man was getting ready in a way that seemed right to him. Both men proceeded to drive the ball off the tee in excess of 300 yards. How people go about preparing themselves for whatever task is before them is a very private and personalized matter.

The issue of the appropriate manner of preparation as a prelude to performance applies to virtually all fields of endeavor. In baseball no two batters get ready to hit in exactly the same way. No two singers warm up before a performance with exactly the same routine. No two teachers prepare their lectures or lesson plans in precisely the same way, even when they are assigned to teach the same subject. How a person prepares to do whatever event or assignment is at hand varies widely from one person to another, even within the same discipline or area of expertise.

The same thing can and must be said about preachers: there is no one right way to prepare a sermon. A variety of steps must be taken and a variety of sources should be consulted, but just how all of that gets woven together into a finished sermon can vary as widely as the preparation for teeing off employed by Tiger Woods and John Daley in that golf tournament. Preachers should feel free to go about sermon preparation in a way that is most efficient and effective for them. Remember, both Tiger Woods and John Daley drove their tee shots more than 300 yards despite their differences in preparation.

The Skill Phase

Joseph Stowell, writing in *Biblical Preaching*, compares sermon preparation to a two-step process leading up to baking a pie. First comes what he calls the "skill phase" and second is the "creative phase." In the skill phase, all shoppers purchase and bring home pretty much the same ingredients for a pie: flour, milk, sugar, shortening, seasonings, and the desired filling. For a sermon, the equivalent ingredients are the results of thorough and reverent biblical exegesis.

In my book *Living Water for Thirsty Souls*, I set forth an eight-step process for doing biblical exegesis for preaching. The first seven of those steps correspond with Stowell's notion of the "skill phase." Step 1 is to *establish limits* on the amount of material to be considered in the sermon. The second step is to *determine what type of biblical literature* is being used. (You would not handle a prophetic text in the same way you would a parable or a proverb.) The third step is careful *study of the language* of the text. This is where the preacher's knowledge of Hebrew and Greek are brought in. Those not fluent in these languages can do a comparative study of three or four different English language versions.

The fourth step is to *consider the physical and social location* in which the text is set. From the tenth century B.C. to the twenty-first century A.D., the world has changed in ways that must be understood when we are trying to apply those ancient texts to our contemporary context. The fifth step *explores links between the passage at hand and other portions of Scripture* in the Old and New Testaments that shed further light on the primary passage. The sixth step entails a *consideration of all the major and minor characters* in the text that offer a point of view from which a sermon might be delivered. This step helps you decide through whose eyes in the text you will interpret the meaning of the passage. The seventh step focuses on *lessons the text offered to the original audience*, whether in Nineveh, Jerusalem, Athens, or Ephesus. The Bible was theirs before it was ours.

The Creative Phase

The eighth step in my approach to sermon preparation—what I call "life application"—corresponds with Stowell's creative phase. Once the exegesis of the text has been completed, there remains the challenge of taking all the information garnered in that process and presenting it in a way that is interesting, informative, and inspiring. This involves matters of structural technique. It is at this point that individuality begins to appear, as each preacher examines the biblical material in light of three distinct factors: (1) the audience to whom the sermon will be preached, (2) the historical and sociopolitical moment in time when the sermon is being prepared and delivered, and (3) the preacher's spiritual and intellectual perspective as informed both by the text and by the times. Because of the variables integral to the creative phase of sermon preparation, there is very little likelihood that any two sermons will be structured the same way—even if preached on exactly the same text on precisely the same date. The ingredients are the same, but they are mixed differently from one person to the next.

The creative phase comprises five steps: (1) an introduction or opening statement, (2) an argument or presentation of the basic claims of the text, (3) illustrations and quotations that might shed light on the points being made, (4) some application of the biblical material to the life and times of people in the congregation, and (5) a conclusion that sums up your basic arguments and points to some appropriate next steps that should be taken by those who have heard the message. How you mix these together and which you pursue first is up to you. However, you would do well to pursue each of the five in your preparation to preach.

Introduction. The two most important sentences in a sermon are the first sentence and the last one. How a sermon begins has great bearing on how likely it is that busy people with a short attention span are going to pay attention to what a preacher says in this most "low-tech" of formats! Even with narrative sermons, an introduction plays an important role in getting people to the story.

The preacher does not have the benefit of pyrotechnic special effects. There is not likely to be a fast-paced slideshow presentation full of colorful graphics. There will certainly be no cheerleaders to root for you as you stand to preach, and there will likely not be any richly designed scenery or set decorations that will help establish the mood of the moment. What the preacher *does* have is a brief amount of time to make a connection between the content of the sermon that has been prepared and the congregation that has gathered on that day.

Many in that congregation have not come explicitly to hear a sermon. Rather, they have come to worship God. For such people the goal of meaningful worship can be achieved as easily through the music offered by the choir or the times of prayer and meditation as it is through the sermon. Remember that just because people are seated in the sanctuary does not mean they are committed to listening to us for the next twenty or thirty minutes. When we stand to preach, we would do well to remember the old adage "You never get a second chance to make a good first impression." What we get is a period of time of two to three minutes to begin a sermon in a way that is interesting and inviting.

Most people have some experience with a television remote control that allows them to surf from one station to another with the push of a button. If what viewers see on one station does not interest them, they do not feel any obligation to stay with that channel simply because they stopped there for a moment. They will push the button and move on in search of something more interesting. Preachers need to understand that people do the same thing as soon as we stand up to preach. Their fingers are already on their mental remote controls, ready to switch to something else if what we have to say does not reach out and grab them.

Of course, people will not get up and walk out of the sanctuary. They may not even fall asleep while we are preaching. They will most likely just begin to drift away into thoughts of dinner, an afternoon outing, or the announcements in the church bulletin they hold in their hands. The best guard against having people change the channel away from our sermons is to get off to a good start through the use of a carefully crafted first sentence that gets people "hooked" or intrigued. The sooner a person listening to a sermon says, "This sounds interesting" or "I want to hear more about this," the better it is for the preacher. The sooner the preacher says something to generate interest or curiosity, the better it is for the listeners.

The purpose of the introduction in a sermon is to hint at the matter to be discussed in the sermon in a way that establishes interest in the topic among the listeners. An introduction ought not to consist of small

talk, pointless anecdotes, or the formalities of acknowl-
edging and greeting the congregation. Nor should it be
confused with the first point in a three-point sermon.
Rather, an introduction is a targeted and intentional act
with one purpose and one purpose only: to establish
interest in the topic for the day and to make a case for
why it is urgent or beneficial for the people gathered
that day to hear what is about to be said.

It is understandable and entirely forgivable if those
who are suddenly called upon to speak without warning or time for preparation seem momentarily flustered
at the beginning of a presentation. They are literally
thinking on their feet. A similar leniency does not
extend to the preacher who has known for several
days—and in some cases for several weeks that a sermon would be expected on a particular day. Approach
your sermon preparation in such a way that from the
very beginning it sounds as if you know exactly where
you are going and why the listeners should go there
with you.

There are a variety of ways by which to shape an
introduction. Most preachers are familiar with another
type of three-point sermon method (beyond the dialectic method discussed in the previous chapter) that consists of the following: (1) Tell them what you are going
to tell them; (2) tell them; and (3) tell them what you
have told them. The first step in this method is the

introduction: "This is what I am going to talk about today, and this is why the text and topic are important." The second step is the presentation of the sermon argument and application. The third step is a reiteration of the message and a reinforcement of the sermon outcome you are hoping to achieve.

Following are some additional options. Keep in mind that no matter the approach taken, a good, solid first sentence is in order.

▪ Begin with a question or observation drawn from the biblical text that offers an angle of vision from which the passage will be considered. Consider something like "I wonder what went through Noah's mind when God told him to build that ark." or "What does it say about life in ancient Jerusalem that only the woman taken in adultery was brought before Jesus and threatened with being stoned? Where was the man?"

▪ Begin with a question or a concern drawn from contemporary society for which the biblical text offers some insight. Consider, "In a world in which arguments about abortion and homosexuality abound, what did Jesus have to say about those two issues?" or "Do you think God is speaking to us and trying to get our attention through all the hurricanes, earthquakes, and tsunamis that have rocked our world recently?"

▪ Begin with stating a problem of personal, congregational, national, or global scale that needs to be solved, suggesting how the text can offer guidance or even a solution to that problem. Consider, "A poll by the Barna Research Institute concluded that 20 percent of the people who attend church every week are addicted to pornography in one form or another" or "Eighty-five years after women received the right to vote in America, they are still denied the right to preach the gospel in many of this country's pulpits."

■ Begin with a quotation taken from your readings or from comments you have heard from others. Consider, "A front-page story in yesterday's newspaper carried this headline: 'Now that Lenin's ideas are dead, what shall we do with his body?'" or "In explaining his conduct with Monica Lewinsky, Bill Clinton wrote these words in his autobiography: 'I did it because I could.'"

■ Begin with a comment that fixes the occasion at which the people have gathered: funeral, church anniversary, Reformation Sunday, Ash Wednesday, or the installation of new lay leaders, to name a few possibilities. When the occasion is clear to the people in the pew, they can all focus on a common event or experience. Consider, "Today is worldwide Communion Sunday, and all around the world our brothers and sisters in Christ are joining us in this remembrance of our Lord's suffering, death, and resurrection" or "It was one hundred years ago today that ten determined people organized this church in one of their homes with nothing more to cling to than their common faith that they were following the leading of the Holy Spirit."

Argument. The argument constitutes the body of the sermon. Several types of argument are rooted in the rhetoric of ancient Greece and Rome and have been adapted for use in debates, as well as in political discourse. Preachers should be aware of them because each of them can easily be employed in the crafting of sermons. Following are some of these forms of argument.

■ *A priori* is an argument that works from cause to effect. This argument states that as a result of a certain act or fact a certain outcome or consequence can be expected. Consider Romans 10:9: "If you confess with your lips that Jesus is Lord and believe in your heart that God raised him from the dead, you will be saved." Or Romans 6:23, which says, "For the wages of sin is death, but the free gift of God is eternal life in Christ Jesus our Lord." Or Judges 21:25, which says, "In those days there was no king in Israel; all the people did what was right in their own eyes." The key to this preaching device is to point out the consequences that follow certain actions. Human behavior can be viewed as a matter of free will, but there are still consequences, both positive and negative, for virtually every action we take in life.

■ *A posteriori* is an argument that works from effect or outcome backward to the cause. It asks why things are the way they are. Arguments that are a part of the raging debate about the origins of the universe are a posteriori arguments. The universe exists with perfect order and unaltered rhythm. Seasons come and go without aid or assistance from us. Why does this happen? How does this occur? What events set this in motion? Some people start with this effect and use the theory of evolution as the initial cause. Others start with the functioning universe and point back to a cause rooted in intelligent design. Still others look at the finished creation and point back to the Creation stories in Genesis 1 and 2 for the cause. The key to this kind of a posteriori argument is to offer an answer to questions about how and why the world or the church or the human condition is in its present shape.

Consider Romans 10:13-17, for example. The effect, or finished product, is stated first: "Everyone who calls on the name of the Lord shall be saved." The text then works backward to explore what causes people to be saved. How can they call on someone in whom they have not believed? How can they believe in someone of whom they have not heard? How can they hear without a preacher? And how can they preach unless they are sent?

■ "Reduction to the absurd" is the kind of argument used to refute the claims of another person by showing that his or her position is either erroneous or injurious if taken to its logical extreme. You might employ humor or sarcasm as you point out the flaws and contradictions in the position against which you are contending. Consider 1 Kings 18:17-40, where Elijah taunts the priests of Baal on Mt. Carmel, or Isaiah's comic discussion of idols in Isaiah 44:13-20, or Paul's sermon in Acts 17 about Jesus while standing amid the statues of the Greek pantheon on Mars Hill in Athens. People in the postmodern world lift up a variety of beliefs, practices, and personalities as alternatives to the gospel of Jesus Christ. Sometimes this more flippant form of argument is the best way to respond to those claims.

■ "Refutation through confrontation" is the most aggressive and forceful form of argument. The best example of this approach to preaching is used by Paul in 1 Corinthians 15:12-22 when he refutes the argument that Christ was not raised from the dead. Paul understood that the resurrection of Jesus was central to the gospel message, and he further understood that he could not allow the idea that the resurrection either did not happen or was not important to take root. Critics of the faith level attacks against doctrines of the faith regarding the nature of Christ or the truth and authority of Scripture. The preacher has a duty to acknowledge that such charges have been made and to defend the faith in the face of those charges.

■ Sometimes the shape of the biblical text may determine the shape of a sermon's argument. In other words, the movements within the Scripture text might be used to determine the points to be made in the sermon. Many times all one needs to do is preach the sermon that is built into the text. The Lord's Prayer, most of the psalms, and many of the proverbs can be preached simply by focusing on one verse or one phrase after another.

However, do not feel obligated to preach all of the verses of a particular chapter or section of Scripture in a single sermon. In fact, this approach to preaching is an excellent way to develop a sermon series (see Section VI for more about sermon series). It allows for the opportunity to go into greater depth in each sermon than would be the case if you tried to squeeze the rich language of, for example, the Lord's Prayer into a single thirty-minute message. The points made earlier in this study concerning expository preaching apply to this approach to preaching (see Section IV, chapter 2). The purpose is to expound upon the biblical text and to make whatever applications may seem appropriate.

Illustrations. The fundamental difference between the preaching/teaching styles of Jesus and Paul is that Jesus made far more use of illustrations as a way to communicate with his audiences. While Paul would go on and on with words and arguments, Jesus was more inclined to talk about the doctrines of grace and salvation by telling a story about a woman who lost a coin and swept her house until she found it, or a shepherd who left ninety-nine sheep to search for the one that was lost, or the father with two sons who welcomed the prodigal back home with a feast and a warm embrace. If asked about the nature of the kingdom of God, Jesus would not try to *explain* it. Rather, he would try to *illustrate* it. He would say the kingdom of heaven is like a sower who went out to sow seeds in a field or like a pearl of great price or like a small amount of leaven in the dough that makes the whole loaf of bread bigger and better.

Jesus did not limit his preaching style to one that depended on the people's ability to reason or to understand his message through words and logic alone. Instead, Jesus told stories that shed light on the point he was trying to make. Any preacher who wants to learn the secret of using illustrations should refer to the parables of Jesus and observe the Master at work. Following are some lessons to be learned by studying Jesus' technique.

1. An illustration should always be employed in service to the larger point being made and not as an end in itself. The illustration brings to life and light the doctrinal or topical issue that is being discussed at that point in the sermon. It might be compared to the illustrations found in children's books that take the form of drawings and sketches that allow the child to "see" what the words on the page are saying. Any parent who has read to a child *Where the Wild Things Are* by Maurice Sendak or *How the Grinch Stole Christmas* by Dr. Seuss or one of the fairy tales of Hans Christian Andersen knows how important those illustrations are in telling the story. It isn't much different with preaching. The illustrations shed light on the major points being discussed. The words *I see* are just as important as the words *I understand*.

2. Jesus employed images and aspects of life with which his audience was familiar in order to illustrate some truth with which they were less familiar. He talked about things with which they could easily identify: a self-righteous Pharisee in the temple, a rich man more concerned with building storage barns than sharing his wealth, a widow who nagged at the king for justice, or a master who left his resources in trust with his servants. No one had to wonder about the language or the images being used; his illustrations were always drawn from within their realm of familiarity.

3. Jesus told stories in such a way as to tap into the imagination and sensory receivers of his audience. He maximized the use of sight, sound, smell, taste, and touch. This appeal to the imagination—and not just to the brain or to the rationale process—is what distinguishes illustration from argument. The whole point is

to allow people to experience in the illustration what is being argued or examined in the sermon. I have often heard great preachers come to the end of a complex portion of their sermon argument and then say, "Let me see if I can bring this thing to life." That is what an illustration should do: bring the thing to life.

Illustrations come easily to those who are paying attention to life. In fact, illustrations can be found wherever you look, and you should try to capture them in writing as soon as they cross your mind. You may overhear something in a conversation that helps shed light on a point in an upcoming sermon. There may be a line from a film, a novel, or a popular song that can illustrate some point you plan to raise. There may be an episode from your own life or the life of someone else, perhaps some well-known character from history, that can serve as a good illustration. Paying attention to roadside billboards and bumper stickers as you travel can also offer great rewards.

Illustrations work best when they are drawn from sources that people are already considering and discussing. We are simply applying snippets from those events and debates in new and interesting ways to shed light on the journey of faith. Keeping up with current events affords you many opportunities to discover events that can illustrate a point in a sermon. Pay attention to the ongoing debates about the place of religion in the public square and to the often conflicting and sometimes coinciding ideas about religion found among Christianity, Islam, Judaism, and other of the world's great religions. Advances in science and medicine, trends in weather patterns and natural disasters, even the home team's winning or losing streak may offer rich potential for sermon illustrations.

Additional illustrations may be gleaned from literary sources, and the more widely a preacher reads, the richer his or her supply of illustrative material will be. William Shakespeare, Langston Hughes, Robert Frost, Alfred Lord Tennyson, Toni Morrison, cartoon strips such as *Peanuts* and *Doonesbury*, the headlines and op-ed pages of the newspaper, national news magazines such as *Time* and *Newsweek*, and faith-based journals such as *Christian Century* and *Christianity Today* are rich resources. So too are product endorsements in commercials, broadcast interviews with newsmakers, quotes from or about sports and entertainment superstars, and the comments of children that so often cut to the heart of issues and questions that concern us all. Much wisdom still proceeds "out of the mouths of babes."

Good illustrations should be captured before they can be forgotten. I am forever indebted to Dr. Ernest Campbell, formerly of Riverside Church in New York City, who emphasized to students at Union Theological

Seminary the virtues of capturing illustrative material as quickly as possible by whatever means available. This may mean tearing something out of the newspaper or a magazine, keeping a small tape recorder handy, carrying a handheld storage device such as a PDA, or writing a quote or comment down on a notepad, a napkin, or some other scrap of paper so the that ideas can be preserved. Whether you prefer high-tech, low-tech, or no-tech, you have sufficient options that no good idea needs to be lost. All the preacher needs is the discipline to capture good illustrations as they come to mind. I have tried to practice this virtue for some thirty years, although it has sometimes called for such extreme measures as pulling my car to the side of the road so I can write something down before I forget it. Do not—I repeat, *do not* trust your memory to recall those sermon illustrations hours after they crossed your mind.

Several additional warnings should be issued about the use of illustrations in sermons.

First and foremost, do not lie or misrepresent the truth in any way. Someone in the audience may know more about the subject than the preacher does. Do not misquote a literary source; there is bound to be a teacher in the audience who knows how it should have been stated. Finally, if you choose to illustrate some point by taking an episode from your own life story, be sure you cast yourself as a mirror of the spiritual problem being discussed, as someone with whom others can identify, not as a model of spiritual rectitude whom others should seek to imitate. Jesus said, "No one is good but God alone" (Mark 10:18), and that includes those of us who preach the gospel!

Sermon Application. Preachers need to make sure that their sermons are not only biblically solid and structurally sound, but also that each message has relevant application to the lives of those who are present to hear it. A sermon is not a lecture where the object is simply to deliver the information with the expectation that the hearers will pick it up and figure out on their own what to do with it. As with a household item that needs to be assembled upon delivery, sermons should come with some instructions for application. In this regard, remember the previously cited four points of application offered by McCracken in *The Making of a Sermon*: kindle the mind, energize the will, disturb the conscience, and stir the heart (see Section III, chapter 2).

Conclusions. All good things must come to an end. This includes a well-crafted sermon. However, the end of that sermon should be as carefully considered as the introduction, the choice of argument, the illustrations, and the application of the sermon to the lives and context of the listeners. Most preachers use the application phase of the sermon as the basis of their conclusion, at least so far as the content of their sermon is concerned. This is perfectly fine, especially if you choose the dialectic method of sermon construction where the sermon ends with the synthesis statement. Of course, if you use the three-point approach of "tell them—tell them—tell them," the third step would also be the conclusion.

The conclusion of a sermon joins the content or subject matter with the sermon's form and style of delivery. It is the fusion of argument and oratory. Rather than simply winding down to a low-key ending, a good sermon should steadily grow and build toward a conclusion that is (1) explosive and joyful as some aspect of the faith is being celebrated, or (2) increasingly intense and poignant as some tragic aspect of the human condition is established as requiring repentance or forgiveness or grace. Like a classical symphony that builds to a triumphant ending or a dramatic movie that carefully steers you to an unexpected encounter with the dark side of human nature, a sermon should not so much *end* as it should *arrive at a destination*.

Every time you are thinking about the conclusion to a sermon, remember what you expect from a movie, television show, or novel as it approaches the end. You do not want an ending that is flat or unimaginative or incapable of moving your mind or your spirit in some way. You want the ending to be exciting, intriguing, captivating, perhaps even surprising, but always effective in tying together everything that has led up to that point.

A solid sermon structure that begins with a compelling introduction, extends to a substantive and well-defined argument, is enhanced by creative illustrations, and is driven home with a relevant application delivered with force and focus can go a long way toward restoring public interest in preaching.

2. Learn to "Play Your Instrument"

Preaching is an oral art form played on the instrument of the human voice. Preachers should learn how to play their instrument as effectively as any singer or instrumentalist. The mastery of oral communication involves the intentional manipulation of the vocal devices of pitch, pace, pause, and volume. These four elements ought to be in evidence throughout the sermon. Vocal variation is the essence of effective speech in all settings, and preachers should work hard to master these four devices. With the possible exception of Louis Armstrong's singing style, oral communication that employs one single note is boring and uninspiring. Of course, while Armstrong was noted for his one-note singing technique, when he played his trumpet he made full use of the variations in pitch, pace, pause, and volume.

Pitch refers to the high and low tones employed while speaking. Variations in pitch guard against a monotone delivery. *Pace* is the variation in the speed or rate at which words are spoken. Here again music becomes the appropriate analogy. No piece of music is set at the fastest or the slowest pace for the entire time. There are moments when the pace is faster or slower. There are times when the music rushes along, and there are times when the pace is slow, emphatic, and deliberate. *Pauses*—those breaks between words or sections or after important quotes—allow the words to be heard with maximum emphasis. When this technique is employed, it is as if every word spoken is heard and considered before the next word or phase is added to the mix. *Volume* should range from the thunderous to just above a whisper. Just as music shifts back and forth and up and down in terms of volume, the same should be true in a sermon. And that vocal variation becomes especially important as the sermon is driving toward its conclusion.

There is a stirring mixture of pitch, pace, pause, and volume as we come to the finale of Beethoven's "Ode to Joy" in the Ninth Symphony, in Mozart's overture to *The Marriage of Figaro*, or in the dramatic third verse of "Lift Every Voice and Sing" by James Weldon Johnson and J. Rosamond Johnson. Those composers played every note available with attention to phrasing, syncopation, and tone. The results speak for themselves. Preachers should think of their voices as musical instruments. We need to explore the ranges that are available to these instruments, and we should play them with as much richness as possible.

"Listen" to the Sermons in Scripture

Imagine Amos preaching in Bethel or John the Baptist preaching in the wilderness or Jesus preaching on the mountainsides of Galilee or Paul preaching on Mars Hill in Athens or before Festus and Agrippa in Caesarea. Imagine Moses preaching before Pharaoh or Elijah on Mt. Carmel as he confronted the priests of Baal. What do you suppose these biblical preachers sounded like as they made their claims for God and for Jesus Christ? Imagine a rich sound defined by pitch, pace, pause, and volume. Then seek that richness in your own preaching—especially as you bring your sermons to a head in the final application or conclusion. Such an ending will help guarantee that your *trumpet will sound a clear call*.

Use of a Manuscript

The final issue that must be addressed regarding sermon design and delivery involves the preparation and use of a manuscript—or to keep with the musical metaphor, the question of whether to play your sermonic song by ear or to follow the notes as written! Few questions are more hotly debated in homiletics (and by preachers themselves) than whether or not a manuscript should be prepared for every sermon, and how and how not to make use of a sermon manuscript during the preaching process. Should a sermon be read word for word from a prepared text? Does the very act of preparing a sermon manuscript in some way appear to "quench" or limit the work of the Holy Spirit as the Spirit moves through the preacher and works in the interaction between the pulpit and the pew?

This issue has positives and negatives on both sides. The benefit of preparing a sermon manuscript is that such a process allows you to think your sermon through to the end. You can work on the structure of the sermon, tinker with the illustrations, insert the desired quotes, and most important of all, review the manuscript over and over in advance of actually preaching the sermon. The negative side of preparing a manuscript resides in the perception that your preaching will appear to be less spontaneous and more like a lecture because you are working from "prepared remarks."

A manuscript also helps you capture your sermon ideas for future use. It is sad to consider how many great sermons by truly great preachers have been lost because those preachers were not in the habit of preparing sermon manuscripts. Today it is possible to capture a sermon on tape or video; thus technology helps us maintain a record of pulpit work. However, this is a record of the *presentation* side of preaching. What a manuscript does is allow us to oversee the *preparation* side of the process. We can study the formation of arguments and the application of the lessons of the biblical passage. Most preachers who are invited to preach away from their home church make use of sermons they have already preached "at home." Having a manuscript for those messages can make your life "on the road" substantially easier.

Having discussed the benefits of preparing a manuscript, the next question is how to *use* that manuscript in the process of delivering a sermon. One does not necessarily have to read from a prepared manuscript when preaching. If the preparation has been thorough enough, one could probably preach the sermon without making any reference to the manuscript. Having done the exegesis of the text, designed the structure of the sermon, and written out the manuscript in full, and having read over and reviewed that manuscript several times (perhaps out loud), that word is probably embedded in your spirit in a way that makes preaching without a manuscript not just possible but fairly easy.

Many people avoid preaching without notes or a manuscript because of one or more fears. They fear they will forget an important point and ruin the sermon. They fear they will misstate a quote or historical fact. They fear their memory will fail them and they will lose their train of thought. To avoid those kinds of eventualities, these preachers not only prepare a full sermon manuscript, but they choose to read from it word for word as well.

Edmund Steimle taught homiletics at Union Theological Seminary in New York City and for years was featured on the weekly National Radio Pulpit broadcast. He offered a keen insight into the use of manuscripts out of the fear of leaving something out of when he said, as he often did, "People will likely never miss what you forget to say, because they never knew it was there to begin with." The tradeoff is between the comfort and reassurance some preachers feel when holding on to a manuscript versus the improved eye contact and freedom of movement that comes with preaching without notes or a manuscript.

Keep in mind that the issue here is not whether to *prepare* a sermon manuscript; the issue is what to do in the pulpit once the manuscript has been prepared. If possible, preach without it so there is nothing before you except the people to whom the sermon is being delivered. If you are not comfortable doing that, then at least avoid the appearance of reading the material by working to sustain as much eye contact as possible with the congregation. The effect of eye contact can be greatly increased if you raise the lectern so that you do not have to look too far down to read from the manuscript. That is, if you can lower your eyes without having to lower your head to see the words, you lessen the impact of working from a manuscript.

There is much middle ground between preparing and preaching from a full manuscript and the extemporaneous style that some preachers prefer, according to which they study and meditate on a biblical text and then preach without any formal structure in mind. Some preachers use tightly written one-page outlines that list their major points, their illustrations, and any specific quotes they want to be sure to state accurately. Some write out the introduction with some care and follow the Spirit from then on. Since many pastors place space in the weekly bulletin for the intended note-taking use of the congregation, preachers might also use this space to jot down a few sermon notes so there is no extra paper visible in the pulpit.

Many preachers labor over trying to memorize their material. This need not be the goal. If the preacher can master the material in the preparation phase, upon standing to preach, he or she will be able to deliver it with power and authority. No matter which form of manuscript use you settle on, do not forget that the function of the sermon is to *sound a clear call*.

Planning a Sermon Series

In the first book, Theophilus, I wrote about all that Jesus did and taught from the beginning until the day when he was taken up to heaven.

—Acts 1:1-2

It is well known that the Acts of the Apostles is a continuation of the Gospel of Luke. One writer is communicating to another person the things Jesus said and did, and it appears that the whole story could not fit into one book. Having covered as much as possible about the life story of Jesus in the Book of Luke, the writer begins the sequel where the first book left off, carrying the story forward into the events that involve the early church and the ministry of the first disciples.

Paul continues this practice of a series or a sequel with 1 and 2 Corinthians, 1 and 2 Thessalonians, and 1 and 2 Timothy. Sequencing, or writing in serial fashion, is in evidence also in the Old Testament with 1 and 2 Samuel, 1 and 2 Kings, and 1 and 2 Chronicles. The epistles of both Peter and John follow a similar pattern.

Over and over again, a certain part the biblical story is divided into two and, in one instance (1, 2, and 3 John), into three separate books because the whole story could not be fully told in one.

Since the Bible consists in part of a series of certain books (sequels, if you will), it should not be surprising when preachers decide to do the same thing in making known the story of Jesus in their own time and place. Among the most valuable skills a preacher can develop is the planning and presentation of a sermon series on some body of biblical material. Rather than overloading one sermon with more information than a congregation can reasonably be expected to absorb in one sitting, the better course of action might be to develop the material into series of two, three, four, or more parts.

Almost inevitably there is more preaching material accrued in the process of exegeting the text and the development of the sermon (skill phase and creative phase) than can be treated thoroughly in any one sermon. A thorough exegesis of virtually any Bible passage will bring to light several different angles from which the text could be examined. Considering the lessons and life application of the text could also result in several different messages from a single text. A preacher will often collect more illustrations than can be used in one sermon as well. One could fairly ask the question, "What shall I do with the *overflow*?"

In the world of filmmaking there are two ways to handle the overflow. One way is to edit out what is not going to be used and leave it "on the cutting room floor." There may have been some great scenes in the initial filming of the movie, but much of it was left out simply because there was more material than could be contained in one film. The other solution is to take what is not going to be used in one film and save it for "the sequel." There are, of course, some instances when the viewing public would have been better off had the original film not been made, let alone the sequel! (The same might be said of some sermons!)

However, there have been some great films that were planned with sequels in mind because no one film could contain all the material that was available. Among the most notable films with sequels are *The Godfather*, *Indiana Jones*, *Rocky*, *Beverly Hills Cop*, *Home Alone*, *The Lord of the Rings*, and *Star Wars*. People can and do debate whether or not some sequels were a good idea. The point is that each of these block-buster films could have stood alone and been memorable in their own right. But the screenwriters and directors realized that the story line could be spread out over two or more films. Rather than leave the overflow of ideas or scenes on the cutting room floor, they decided to develop the plot and the characters in a series of equally interesting and entertaining motion pictures.

The concept of starting with a basic premise or area of interest and developing an initial offering into a series extends beyond film to the world of novels and stage plays. John Grisham began his examination of the world of lawyers and courtroom intrigues with *The Firm*. There was obviously more material he wanted to deal with than could be squeezed into that one novel, so he subsequently wrote other equally compelling works, including *The Pelican Brief*, *A Time to Kill*, and *The Client*. The playwright August Wilson wanted to do a series exploring the culture and conditions of African Americans. This ended up as a ten-part cycle that included *Ma Rainey's Black Bottom* and *Fences*, both of which won him a Pulitzer Prize.

1. Start with the Lectionary

Like the writer or filmmaker, the preacher can get maximum use from material uncovered in preparing for an initial sermon by creating a series in which each week's message builds on the foundation laid the week before. The material uncovered in the initial exegesis can be used in various ways over an extended period of time. As a matter of course, the preacher should look to see if any selected text or topic could become part of a sermon series. This approach to planning and preparation is not only efficient in terms of time and effort, but it can also result in some very creative preaching, as characters, contexts of action, and theological content can be more carefully unpacked and examined.

Perhaps the best and simplest method for developing a sermon series is to follow a lectionary. The virtues and value of the lectionary itself were discussed earlier in this book (see Section III, chapter 1). Those who make use of a lectionary already know the benefits of a sermon series because the weekly readings assigned by the lectionary are designed to lead you through several books of the Bible in systematic fashion. Thus, the preacher is automatically doing a sermon series on, for example, Exodus, Psalms, Matthew, or Philippians.

2. Use the Expository Method

The second best way to approach a sermon series is to employ the expository methodology in analyzing a single portion of Scripture, typically a doctrinal or theological matter, over a series of weeks. Harold Bryson, in his book *Expository Preaching*, writes, "Expository preaching is the art of preaching a series of sermons, either consecutive or selective from a Bible book."[1] A thorough, line-by-line study of a text and, in many instances, a word-by-word analysis can supply material for several sermons and can result in a rich learning experience.

Start out with familiar passages of Scripture, passages that people may have heard in a sermon in their whole form, but most likely have never considered in a line-by-line or word-by-word fashion. For instance, do an expository sermon series on passages such as the blessing of Aaron in Numbers 6, the Twenty-third Psalm, John 3:16-17, the Lord's Prayer, or 1 Corinthians 13. Great expository preaching material may be found in Philippians 4:8 where Paul says, "Finally, beloved, whatever is true, whatever is honorable, whatever is just, whatever is pure, whatever is pleasing, whatever is commendable, if there is any excellence and if there is anything worthy of praise, think about these things." Any lengthy passage that offers variety in terms of words, concepts, characters, or doctrinal statements can be approached as expository in its structure and has great potential as a sermon series.

The Bible includes several small books as well as books with a biographical focus that are strong candidates for a sermon series. One could begin with the dramatic stories found in Ruth and Esther, as well as in Ezra and Nehemiah. Jude and 3 John both deserve attention, but one sermon would usually not provide enough time. Those who use the lectionary already know how easy a sermon series on Psalms can be, and those who select their texts in a more random manner might want to consider a series on certain types of psalms, including praise, contrition, comfort, and royal. The truly daring might consider a series on the longest psalm of all: Psalm 119.

Most of the epistles of the New Testament can be approached in series fashion. The ministry of Jesus could also be treated in a sequential manner: birth and childhood narratives, the Galilean phase of his life, the events in Judea, the Passion narrative, the four resurrection stories in the Gospels, the Great Commission language in Matthew and Mark, and finally the ascension scenes in Luke–Acts.

3. Base It on "Multiples"

A third way to plan a sermon series is to focus on those aspects of the biblical story that in some way come in multiples. Consider planning a sermon series on each of the Ten Commandments or each of the Beatitudes. A series could be planned around the parables spoken or the miracles performed by Jesus. Study the sermons and sayings of Paul in his prison epistles or the benedictions that occur at the end of so many of Paul's other letters. Consider the unique messages spoken by the Holy Spirit to the seven churches of Asia Minor in the Book of Revelation. Preachers should also consider the seven "I Am" sayings of Jesus that are scattered throughout the Gospel of John. At the other end of the emotional spectrum would be a series on the harsh and vivid "woe statements" in Matthew 23 that Jesus directs against the religious leaders of his time. Many warnings are found there that we in the twenty-first century church could profit from hearing.

Study and examine the content of the prayers and the prayer habits of Jesus. Introduce your listeners to the divergent group of women who appear in the New Testament and who in some way influence the ministries of Jesus and Paul. And, for those who have not already done so, it is long past time for sermons to break the silence concerning the presence of African people in the Bible, especially as they appear in the life of the early church, as recounted in Acts 10 and 13.

4. Choose a Rich Scripture Passage

A fourth way to approach a sermon series is to develop several sermons around a single passage or chapter of the Bible, moving from one set of verses to the next. The idea of a sermon series or sequels to an initial sermon was the premise for the sermons contained in my book *Living Water for Thirsty Souls*, which included a Lenten series of eight messages based on the characters, comments, and conditions that surrounded Jesus during the crucifixion, as described in Luke 23. That one chapter provided angles of vision that made the story of the crucifixion fresh and new from week to week, because the same events were being considered from varying points of view. The Pharisees standing at the foot of the cross saw things differently from the Roman soldiers who were part of the execution squad. However, one centurion who announced at the end of the ugly process that Jesus was the Son of God seemed to see things differently from his cohorts.

The crowd that gathered in Pilate's courtyard clamoring for the death of Jesus held a different view of Jesus than did that Roman governor. Herod's and Barabbas' viewpoints offer very different perspectives on the claim that Jesus was the King of the Jews. The sudden appearance of a man from North Africa named Simon of Cyrene, who is compelled to carry Jesus' cross, adds greater texture to this international cast of characters. There were three crosses on Calvary that day, and each was occupied by a different person, each of whom had distinctive reasons for being there. We do not know much about the other two men who died alongside Jesus, but we do know they could not agree about the identity of this man who was dying on center stage at Calvary that day.

What did the members of the Sanhedrin think when the body of Jesus was claimed by Joseph of Arimathea, a member of the ruling elite? What can be said about any expectation of resurrection on the part of those women who were prepared to anoint the body of Jesus for proper burial as soon as the Sabbath had ended?

In addition to inviting an analysis of these varying points of view, this single biblical chapter also provides us with an in-depth look at the character of Jesus during those traumatic hours. During his trial before

Pontius Pilate, Jesus seemed to confirm the primary charge leveled against him, namely, that he could rightly be called "king of the Jews." Just a verse or two later, Jesus refused to speak even one word to Herod. On his way to Calvary, Jesus spoke to some people who were weeping over his fate, telling them it was *he* who felt sorry for *them* because of the trials awaiting them as a result of the sins of their generation. In one of his trademark moments, while under intense pressure and physical pain, Jesus was yet able to quote to them a passage of Scripture (Hosea 10:8).

Beyond all these comments and conversations, this same chapter contains three of the seven sayings spoken by Jesus from the cross: "Father, forgive them; for they do not know what they are doing," "Today you will be with me in Paradise," and "Father, into your hands I commend my spirit." If ever there was a lesson taught about how to face death with faith in God and without a word of self-pity or regret, this is that lesson. Those three words from the cross could occupy a creative preacher and captivate a congregation for many weeks.

Reactions to the death of Jesus are visible in the crowd. As already mentioned, there was the centurion who praised God and announced that Jesus really was the Son of God. Then there were those bystanders who had come to observe the crucifixion, much like people in nineteenth- and twentieth-century America who actually gathered to watch and witness a lynching of another human being. When Jesus died, that group "beat their breasts" as a sign of remorse or regret over the actions that had just been concluded, and then they went away. Finally, the text speaks of "all his acquaintances, including those women who had followed him from Galilee," who stood at a distance watching the events unfold. Who was in that group? Was it Peter and John and other disciples? Was it Mary his mother and Mary Magdalene? They had followed him from Galilee, according to Luke 23:49, and it is certain this was not the outcome they were expecting, especially when they considered the reception Jesus had received when he rode into Jerusalem just five days earlier.

This is one example out of dozens scattered throughout the Bible in which one passage, rich in *characters*, *conversations*, and cultural, social, and political *contexts*, can offer widely differing ways from which to read and react to the same material. The key to doing this effectively is learning how to pay attention to the Bible as story and to the developments of the plot in that story. There are as many ways to preach a text as there are voices heard, persons present, or doctrinal and theological issues at stake in that one passage of Scripture. Most of this material is left "on the cutting room floor" when preachers try to handle in a single sermon all the information they have uncovered in their exegesis and preparation.

No one would read a tragedy by William Shakespeare and conclude that the great English bard had included even one character or one scene from which nothing essential to the plot could be extracted. We examine the words, the motives, and the actions of every character in *Hamlet* or *Macbeth* or *Othello*. As compelling as the histories, tragedies, and comedies of Shakespeare may be, in truth even his writings are no match for the storytelling skills of the biblical writers. There is a reason why the gospel is called "the greatest story ever told." Preachers should familiarize themselves with every detail of that story, and especially those aspects of the story present in the text they are using as the basis for a sermon. Do not speed up your analysis of the text so you can make your point in one rushed, generalized, and overburdened sermon. Instead, slow down so you can carefully and intentionally call to the attention of your listeners everything the biblical writers placed there for our consideration.

5. Walk with the Disciples of Jesus

A fifth approach to developing a sermon series might be to examine the lives and lessons that can be learned from the Lord's original twelve disciples. This approach would expose listeners to a much wider range of Scripture while maintaining a fairly narrow focus so far as the subject matter is concerned. There is ample material dealing with Peter, James, and John, and there are some interesting possibilities that await a consideration of the other nine.

Consider the sociopolitical tensions that must have existed from the start when Jesus in Luke 6:14-16 called both Matthew the tax collector and Simon the Zealot to be his disciples. Tax collectors raised money from Jews to support the Roman army that occupied the Jewish nation of Judea. Zealots were religious radicals who were the sworn enemies of Rome and who sought to be delivered from Roman domination by any means necessary. Here is material for sermons dealing with diversity and tolerance and conflict resolution in the family of faith.

It seems that Philip was a central character when it came to bringing people to Jesus or to a wider knowledge of his message. In John 1:43-46 it was Philip who told Nathaniel that he had found the Messiah: Jesus of Nazareth. When Nathaniel scornfully replied, "Can anything good come out of Nazareth?" Philip responded with the invitation to "come and see." In John 12:20-22, it was Philip who was approached by some Greeks who asked him to introduce them to Jesus. This resulted in one of the most compelling sayings of Jesus: "And I, when I am lifted up from the earth, I will draw all people to myself" (12:32). In Acts

8:26-40 it was Philip who encountered an Ethiopian and converted him to faith in Christ.

There are powerful stories and potential lessons in Scripture involving many of the other disciples. It was Andrew who introduced his brother Simon to Jesus. Lesson: We never know what God might do with the people we introduce to Jesus. We criticize absent Thomas for not believing the report given to him by the other disciples about Jesus' resurrection appearance. Lesson: We call him "Doubting Thomas" disparagingly, but would we have acted differently and believed that unbelievable report without the kind of confirmation being sought by Thomas?

Several passages dealing with Judas Iscariot help us get a broader understanding of this infamous character. What is the essential difference between Judas, who betrayed Jesus one time, and Peter, who denied Jesus three times? Could Judas have received the Lord's forgiveness if he, like Peter, had remained alive until resurrection morning when the angel said, "Go, tell the disciples and Peter that he is going ahead of you to Galilee"? What happens when preaching points out that, so far as our daily lives are concerned, most Christians are far more like Judas than they are like Jesus?

What should we make of the fact that most of the Lord's first disciples were never, after they had been chosen, referenced singularly in the Gospels or Acts?

What stories revolve around Bartholomew or Thaddeus or the other Judas (the son of James)? In this age when preachers are preoccupied with celebrity and fame, it is interesting to note that the first preachers of the gospel were committed to being faithful without being concerned about being famous. This would extend to Matthias, the disciple who replaced Judas Iscariot (Acts 1:23-26). Even less is known about him, although he met all the qualifications to *become* a disciple and probably ran all the risks of *being* a disciple.

A series on the disciples of Jesus could extend beyond the original Twelve plus Matthias by considering those whose ministry was essentially postresurrection. This would begin with the life of Paul and would include Barnabas, John Mark, Silas, Phoebe, Demas, Priscilla and Aquila, Timothy, Apollos, Tychicus, and of course, Luke, the beloved physician. Each of these persons, and many others who could be considered, offer important insights into the missionary work of the church.

6. Consider Other Groups of Bible Characters

A sermon series on Bible characters might extend to the men and women who served as judges in Israel in the years before the establishment of the monarchy. A series on the world and words of the prophets would be as informative about biblical history as it would be instructive in the elements of biblical faith set forth by the prophets over a two-hundred-year period. The sovereignty of God is reinforced every time God seems to be moving through or exercising dominion over foreign kings mentioned in the Bible, ranging from the pharaohs of Egypt to Nebuchadnezzar in Babylon, from Cyrus and Darius of Persia to Augustus Caesar of Rome. Speaking of Rome, a series could also be done on the Romans and how their lives were influenced by the life and teachings of Jesus. That would include the centurion in Luke 7:6 who asked Jesus to heal his servant; the centurion at Calvary in Matthew 27:54 who declared that Jesus was the Son of God; Cornelius, the centurion who received a vision about Peter in Acts 10; and Julius, the centurion in Acts 27 who kept Paul from being killed following a shipwreck on the way to Rome. It seems that long before Emperor Constantine was converted to Christianity, many Romans had already been touched by the gospel message and its messengers.

There are also many wonderful possibilities for a series on the children or young people in the New Testament, ranging from the boy in John 6:8 whose lunch was used to feed the multitudes in Galilee, to the daughter of Jairus who was raised from the dead (Mark 5:41), to Eutychus of Troas who was restored to life by Paul after he fell from a third-story window (Acts 20:9).

7. Explore the Names and Attributes of God

One way to help people grasp the nature and character of God is to offer a sermon series examining the texts that speak to the many names and associated attributes of God found in the Bible. One series could focus on the attributes of *omnipotence*, *omniscience*, and *omnipresence*. Great comfort can be offered by reminding people of the availability and the sufficiency of God's power, God's knowledge and wisdom, and God's sovereignty and universal presence in all of creation. There is also much to be learned about God by focusing on the list of "Jehovah" names scattered throughout the Old Testament. They are *Jehovah Jireh* (The Lord Will Provide), found in Genesis 22:14; *Jehovah Nissi* (The Lord Is My Banner), found in Exodus 17:15; *Jehovah Shalom* (The Lord Is Peace), found in Judges 6:24; *Jehovah Shammah* (The Lord Is There), found in Isaiah 60:14-22; and *Jehovah Tsidkenu* (The Lord Is Our Righteousness), found in Jeremiah 23:6 and 33:16.

A similar series could be planned around the names and titles ascribed to Jesus in the New Testament. Explore the historical and theological meanings of such names and titles as Messiah, Christ, Son of David, Son of Man, Son of God, King of the Jews, Savior, and Lamb of God. Each of these names offers a different insight into the character and ministry of Jesus and into the historical context in which that ministry took place. Such a sermon series would shed light on all four Gospels, on various aspects of biblical theology, and especially on the issue of continuity and discontinuity, which helps people understand what material from the Old Testament does and does not cross over into the New Testament.

8. Delve into Controversial Issues

What does the Bible teach us about marriage? What is the role of women in the church? What does Jesus have to say on the topic of homosexuality? How does stem cell research infringe on God's roles as creator and healer? Is it proper, after September 11, 2001, for a Christian to embrace pacifism and reject war? This is just a sampling of questions that are being debated in society in general and in the church in particular. Any one of them could constitute a fascinating sermon series.

Is Jesus Christ the only path to salvation? If so, what will happen to the souls of our devout Jewish and Muslim friends who do not confess that Christ is Lord? Is the separation of church and state in conflict with the sovereignty of God? Should a secular, democratic nation use the words "One nation under God" in its national pledge of allegiance? Why are there so many different denominations and so many subgroups within almost every denomination? These are the questions that many in our pews are asking, and we would do well to give those questions careful consideration. A sermon series is one way to approach these matters.

Although it may not qualify as "controversial," liberation theology certainly is new ground for most people sitting in our pews—and even for many preachers in the pulpit. Although much has been written about liberation theology over the last thirty years, only a few of those writings, such as *Preaching Liberation* by James Harris and *Liberation Preaching* by Justo and Catherine Gonzalez, have applied this thinking to the work of preaching. A very useful sermon series could be preached on the various Bible texts that have been invoked by liberation theologians. This genre of theology would encompass black theology, feminist theology, womanist theology, and the liberation theology movements found in Latin America and throughout Asia and Africa.

Such a series could include Exodus 19 and the story of the Hebrew exodus from slavery that was the basis for James Cone's approach to black theology. Attention could then be given to the Luke 4 passage where Jesus cited Isaiah 61 and declared that he had come to "set at liberty those who are oppressed." The Luke passage, which would make for a wonderful series on its own, also focuses on the fact that God's love and concern extend beyond any one nation to all the nations of the earth. Another possibility is Paul's reflection in Galatians 3:28, which speaks about there being no difference between male and female, Jew and Gentile, and slave and free in Christ Jesus.

Much is to be gained through a sermon series. A careful approach to the analysis of biblical material can greatly increase Bible knowledge among those who have ears to hear. A well-planned and well-advertised sermon series can also establish enough interest in the congregation that attendance may increase and remain stable as people return week after week to see how the story unfolds. In other words, "To Be Continued" need not apply only to TV programs; it can work just as well in the pulpits of careful and creative preachers.

Note
1. Harold T. Bryson, *Expository Preaching: The Art of Preaching through the Bible* (Nashville: Broadman & Holman, 1999), p. 39.

Sermon Outlines

The following sermon outlines provide guidance related to sermon themes and purpose, relevant Scripture texts, content and illustrations, delivery, and desired outcome. In most instances, the items that follow "For Your Consideration" are specific suggestions for adapting the sermon content to the individual preacher's context. However, some of these items relate more to questions the preacher might consider while preparing the sermon. It is hoped that these outlines will be useful not only in their own right, but also as illustrative tools for preachers to develop their own outlines and sermons.

A Living Sacrifice
For a Communion Service
Text: Rom. 12:1-2
Supporting Texts: John 1:36; 3:3; 2 Cor. 5:17

Theme and Purpose
This sermon could be used to encourage people to move away from the rituals of the religious life and to

engage in concrete actions that are an expression of their life of faith.

Sermon Content

Introduction: Paul began with an urgent plea found nowhere else in his writings: "I beseech you" or "I plead with you." What is of such urgency that Paul felt the need to *beg* people to pay attention? This question becomes the initial point of interest in the introduction that leads to the body of the sermon.

Point 1: Paul was mindful of the religious practice of animal sacrifice that was common in so many of the religions of the first century, but especially in Judaism. Paul wanted to have Christians break with that practice and with the thinking and behavior associated with it. Animal sacrifice did not require a change in behavior, and it left those making the sacrifice feeling that they had lived up to all of their religious duties. Paul, like Jesus in the Sermon on the Mount, wanted to call Christians beyond the letter of the law to a far higher and deeper principle: transformed lives. Do not sacrifice an animal; sacrifice the sin so that repeated animal sacrifices are no longer necessary.

Point 2: Another fundamental difference between a living sacrifice and an animal sacrifice is the number of times it can be offered. You can offer an animal sacrifice only once, but a living sacrifice can be offered in service to God over and over again. There are people who are willing to make a sacrifice of some sort once in their lives, whether it is a sacrifice of time, money, or service in some leadership position. However, having made it once, they are not willing to repeat that sacrifice. They think they have "paid their dues" to the church for the year. Paul was calling on Christians to stop keeping count of what they have done for Christ and to be willing to serve, sacrifice, and even suffer over and over again for the cause of the kingdom of God.

Point 3: The goal toward which Paul was pointing is not just that Christians should go through the rituals of their religion (baptism, Communion, worship, etc.), but that their lives should become wholly transformed by their encounter with Jesus Christ. His words of challenge were: "Do not be conformed to this world, but be transformed by the renewing of your minds." The objective of our encounter with Christ is transformation. Jesus calls it being "born again" (see John 3:3). In 2 Corinthians 5:17, Paul referred to it as being "a new creation." Either way you look at it, our relationship with Jesus Christ remains immature and unfinished unless and until our minds, our hearts, our values, and our behavior have all been transformed and brought into conformity with the Lord's perfect will for our lives. Anything less than this is offering God a one-time animal sacrifice and not a lifelong living sacrifice.

Dr. Martin Luther King Jr. coined the phrase "transformed non-conformists" in which he called upon people never to conform to any aspect of the world that was unkind, unjust, or unfair to any person. That is what Paul is calling for in this passage—that we no longer conform to the patterns and prejudices of this world. Instead, we ought to allow our lives to be so transformed by the teachings of the gospel that we really do become born-again, new creations.

Point 4: There is a final reason why we should abandon the practice of animal sacrifice beyond the fact that we should make living sacrifices of our lives. Animal sacrifices are no longer needed. The last and all-sufficient sacrifice for sin has already been made. Jesus is the Lamb of God who takes away the sins of the world (see John 1:36). He was our sacrifice. His blood covered our sins. By his stripes we are healed. We should become living sacrifices in obedience to the one who became our atonement sacrifice on the cross at Calvary.

Sermon Delivery

This sermon would work well as a narrative sermon where the preacher tells the story of first-century Jewish religious practice centering on temple sacrifices. From that starting point, and recognizing that Paul wanted to define the fundamental differences between Judaism and the teachings of Jesus Christ, the distinctions between the animal and the living sacrifices can then be drawn.

Sermon Outcome

What the preacher is intending here is for the hearers of this sermon to have their consciences disturbed about their present religious practice, and also to be energized to assume the role of living sacrifices in their ongoing relationship with Christ.

For Your Consideration

1. Identify any religious traditions and routines in your local church that have become forms of "animal sacrifice" by which people are going through the motions of religion rather than wholeheartedly devoting themselves to Christ and to the work of the kingdom.

2. What acts of personal sacrifice or service have you or the members of your congregation been willing to do for Christ "only once"? What limits, if any, have you placed on your availability to the service of God?

3. Consider the environment in which you and your congregation exist. What kind of nonconformity with existing values, beliefs, and prejudices are required of Christians in the community where you live?

4. How do you relate to people who continually apologize to God for ungodly behaviors and attitudes that they have no intention of abandoning?

The Value of a True Vine

For the Season of Lent
Text: John 15:1-8
Supporting Text: Ps. 91:1

Theme and Purpose

This sermon is designed to make the point that we as Christians must have solid and continuing points of contact with Jesus Christ in order for our relationship with him to remain strong and vibrant. The text calls upon us to "abide in the vine." The sermon swings on the distinction between *abiding* and other words that imply a less meaningful relationship, words such as *attending, affiliating,* or *associating* with the vine.

Sermon Content

Point 1: The church needs to be challenged about its lax and inconsistent connection to God. Too many Christians come to church at their "convenience" and only when it suits their schedule. If there is something else scheduled during a time for worship or for the business of the church, they are quite content to turn aside from God until a more convenient time. At the same time, they want and expect God to hear and answer their prayers as soon as the last words of the prayer have been spoken. They do not abide or remain in God, but they expect God to abide with them. Jesus told us it does not work that way.

Christians need to understand that we need God far more than God needs us. The branch is dependent on the vine, not vice versa. God can always find somebody else to do what we fail or refuse to do because of our sense of apathy or self-importance. Where else can *we* turn to access what God provides to us? Jesus said, "I am the vine and you are the branches, and without me you can do nothing."

Point 2: When we recognize our role as a branch, several things about branches become object lessons for us. The first is that no two branches are the same, just like no two leaves or roses or plants of any kind are the same. God is the master of diversity in creation: many shapes, many sizes, and many colors. We need to learn the lesson of diversity from God so that our churches can learn to value people who look different and may do things differently, but who bring many fresh gifts to the body of Christ.

One of the gifts God has given to the church is the gift of variety when it comes to styles of worship and preaching. Those raised on sacred anthems have no room for gospel music. Those accustomed to a one-hour worship service do not understand why anyone would still be in church after two and a half hours. If we had a little more Jesus and a little less jealousy in us, we could better appreciate one another. As long as we are equally tied to the vine, it should not matter if our respective branches look a little different from one another.

Point 3: Branches do not have to work hard at producing the proper fruit or leaves. When they are attached to the vine, they produce whatever fruit is appropriate. We as Christians should be producing the fruits of the Spirit as found in Galatians 5:22-23. We cannot do this unless we are abiding in the vine. Gardner Taylor once said, "Cut flowers look good, but they do not last very long." The same is true with "cut Christians." The more disconnected we are from the vine, the harder it will be to bear good fruit. The closer we are to the source of our power, the easier it will be to bring forth fruit.

The body employs two kinds of movement or motion—voluntary and involuntary. Voluntary movements are those that we plan or choose to do: stand up, sit down, raise or lower a hand or a voice. Involuntary movements are the ones that happen automatically and without any need to direct them into action. Our eyes blink, our hearts beat, our lungs contract without our having to remind them to do so. Our practice of faith should move from the voluntary to the involuntary, from manual to automatic without any need to "shift into action."

Point 4: Jesus observed that sometimes a gardener has to prune a plant or a tree in order for it to bear more fruit. The same principle is true in our relationship with God. Sometimes God has to prune us in order for us to bear more fruit. The sicknesses and setbacks and sorrows we experience in life are not to be understood as God turning away from us. Instead, God is very often orchestrating every move as he prunes us so we can bear even more fruit.

Point 5: One final benefit of being tied to a vine is that the vine can hold the branch when strong winds begin to blow. If the connection is not strong, branches will be torn away from the tree. However, if we are abiding in the vine, we may bend but we will not break away because the strength of the vine is holding us fast. Many are the times when all we will have to hold on to is the strength of the vine. Our own arms will be too short. Our own minds will be too limited. But if we can just "hold on and hold out," the vine will keep us until the storm has passed over.

Sermon Delivery

This is an expository sermon where the language and movement of the text provides the structure of the sermon. The motif of the relationship between a vine and a branch unlocks the imagination for the points that need to be made.

Sermon Outcome

The desired outcome of this sermon would be to kindle the mind and to stir the heart. The mind is kindled when we think about how we are abiding in the vine currently and how life may become different, better, more successful, and secure when our connection is as strong as possible. Our hearts are stirred to rejoice when we are reminded that in the time of storm it is the vine that will hold us up and carry us through whatever the crisis of the moment might be.

For Your Consideration

1. Cite and address some of the challenges of diversity —racial, economic, generational, theological, physical, etc.—that confront your local church or your local community.

2. List some of the ways God has "pruned" you so that your ministry could bear more fruit. Has it been a sickness, a career setback, or perhaps a crisis in your family? What fruits did you see as a result?

3. What "works of the flesh" do the people in your congregation need to guard against? What "fruits of the Spirit" do you see at work in the life of your church?

4. Describe the experiences in your life that cause you to say with the hymn writer, "Through many dangers, toils, and snares I have already come."[1]

Four Dimensions of the Love of God

For Valentine's Day
Text: Eph. 3:14-19
Supporting Texts: Ps. 139; Matt. 7:24-27; John 16:33; Rom. 8:37-39; 1 John 4:20

Theme and Purpose

In verse 19, Paul spoke of knowing the love of God that surpasses knowledge. How can one *know* something that is beyond *knowledge*? That is the problem or tension in the text. The answer is that some things can be known only by experiencing them for oneself. This sermon addresses how the love of God is known by experiencing its height, depth, breadth, and length.

Sermon Content

Introduction: There are a great many things in life that cannot be known solely through human reason and understanding. You cannot "know" food without experiencing its taste. You cannot "know" a new car without experiencing its smell and sight and feel. You cannot "know" any form of love between people without experiencing it through the words and deeds that bring love to life. Human life is not lived entirely at the level of the cerebral where everything must be comprehended and understood, proven and tested. Some things can be truly known only when we experience them. This is even truer when it comes to our relationship with God, which is not so much understood as it is experienced.

My parents had a favorite phrase whenever they were about to discipline my brother and me for some infraction of their rules. Realizing that their words must have fallen on deaf ears as far as understanding was concerned, they would say, "I can show you better than I can tell you." That is the way it is with God's love. It is as if God is saying to us, "I can show you better than I can tell you." We know God's love when we encounter God in the height and depth and breadth and length of God's actions in our lives.

Point 1: The love of God has a height to it, an ability to lift us up from where we are to a higher level of faith, hope, joy, and love. The love of God also reveals to us the inexhaustible love that God has for fallen, lost, and disobedient humanity. One hymn writer said, "From sinking sand he lifted me."[2] All believers should be able to note the spiritual growth they have experienced since their conversion. God wants us to grow up and mature in our faith. It is God's desire for us to look back on the life we were living and realize how far the Lord has brought us since the day we first believed.

Point 2: We experience the depth of the love of God when we realize how our lives can be anchored and grounded in Christ in ways that allow us to be sustained when we pass through times of testing, turmoil, and tribulation. If we build our lives on a firm foundation as Jesus urged in Matthew 7:24-27, then we will be able to stand in the face of the wind and the waves and in the face of the rain that falls and beats against our lives. In John 16:33, Jesus said, "In the world you face persecution. But take courage; I have conquered the world!"

Point 3: The breadth of the love of God hints at the ways God attempts to stretch us beyond our comfort level and challenge us to embrace and affirm and accept people we may formerly have hated or rejected for reasons of race, gender, ethnicity, or lifestyle. God's love extends to everyone, and God wants our love to be equally inclusive, equally broad. If there is room for *us* in God's heart, then we should be willing to make room for others in our hearts. Issues of oppression and discrimination may be addressed from this perspective. As 1 John 4:20 observes, "Those who say, 'I love God,' and hate their brothers or sisters, are liars; for those who do not love a brother or sister whom they have seen, cannot love God whom they have not seen."

"Eleven a.m. Sunday morning is the most segregated hour in America." Why do those words of Liston Pope

from 1960 remain true in 2006? Why are most church-
es in America marked by their astounding homogene-
ity? On the Day of Pentecost, people were gathered
from every region of the earth to hear Peter declare the
message of the gospel. Today we have retreated into
enclaves and islands of racial, ethnic, theological, and
ideological sameness. We desperately need the breadth
of God's love to stretch us until our arms are opened
wide enough to welcome and receive all our brothers
and sisters in Christ.

Point 4: Every human relationship we experience
operates within the limits of time and space. No matter how much we love someone, death or distance may
separate us. Not so with the love of God. There is no
distance that can separate us from the love of God.
Psalm 139 reminds us of the long reach of God's love.
Romans 8:38-39 assures us that *nothing* can separate
us from the love of God. Not even death can prevent
the love of God from reaching us. This is the meaning
and the message of the resurrection. God's love sustains
us not only unto death, but also into life eternal.

Anyone who has ever walked away from a cemetery,
leaving behind the body of a loved one, knows all too
well how quickly that kind of love can be snatched
away. Similarly, many people know what it is like to
have someone they loved decide to walk out on them

with little or no warning. My own father walked out on his family when I was ten years old. That experience reminds us that our human efforts at love can be uncertain and unreliable.

Sermon Delivery

This is an instance in which the shape of the text can become the shape of the sermon. The question about how we can know God's love is answered as each of these four dimensions of God's love is experienced. Simply by moving from one form to the next, the message of the sermon unfolds. Each step calls for a different level of response from the audience. The first three points challenge and encourage listeners in specific areas. The fourth point is a word of celebration as it reminds us of the unending reach of God's love.

Sermon Outcome

This sermon can stir the heart of all believers as they understand by experience what they could never understand by reasoning: the height, depth, breadth, and length of God's love. This sermon should also disturb the conscience of those whose love does not extend very far as a result of some prejudice or hatred. As a result of this sermon, people should be challenged to act out this principle of broadening the scope and reach of their love and concern toward others.

For Your Consideration
1. In what ways do people in your congregation need to "grow up" and mature as Christians?
2. What experiences of being sustained in and delivered from some difficulty come to mind that illustrate the depth of the love of God? Consider sharing one or more as a sermon illustration.
3. In what ways are you personally challenged by the breadth of the love of God? Are there any people, whether individuals or groups, whom you are still unable or unwilling to love and to embrace? How does this same question apply to the life of your local church and to your neighbors and friends?
4. Are there people in your church who have recently lost a loved one? If so, consider some words from the pulpit that might continue to assist them as they make their way "through the valley of the shadow of death."

One Life Can Make a Difference

For New Year's Sunday or Martin Luther King Jr. Day
Text: 1 Sam. 17:8-11, 50-52

Theme and Purpose

This sermon should remind people at the beginning of the year that how they live their lives has the potential to make a difference in shaping or reshaping events, both locally and globally.

Sermon Content

Introduction: Some scholars have asserted that history is not just a series of events, but an analysis of the people who do three things: (1) face a great problem, (2) confront the problem despite the personal risk they may encounter, and (3) do this despite the fact that others have already passed on the opportunity to do the same. All three conditions must be present in order for a so-called great person to emerge. Thus, this approach to history is called "The Great Person Theory."

Winston Churchill strengthened Great Britain to stand up to Hitler and the Nazis in 1940. Mohandas Gandhi strengthened India to stand up to Churchill and the British colonial government. George Washington held the newly formed United States together during the revolutionary years from 1776–1781. Rosa Parks initiated a massive culture shift not only in this country, but in countries all over the world. And a boy named David made a difference in the life of his nation when he went out to fight the Philistine giant named Goliath.

Point 1: When Goliath challenged the army of Israel with the freedom and future of the nation hanging in the balance, he posed a great problem. Anyone who was willing to go out and confront him in single combat would be facing a great risk. David was willing to go despite the fact that no one in the army, including his own older brothers, had been willing to accept the challenge from Goliath. David exhibited the characteristics of greatness when he faced a great problem, ran a great risk, and did what others who were older and more experienced in combat were unwilling to attempt.

Point 2: David's faith and courage resulted in more than his personal victory over Goliath. His actions also emboldened the rest of the Israelite army, who attacked the Philistines as soon as Goliath had been killed. The future of Israel, which been very much in doubt, was now secure as a result of the faith and courage of one person whose life made a difference. One minute the entire army of Saul was frozen in fear at the prospects that confronted them: not just a military defeat but also a return to slavery. The next minute, the army was "surging forward" in an attack that helped seal their freedom for centuries to come. One life can make a difference.

Point 3: Most people can think of one or more persons beyond their immediate family who made a difference in their lives—a teacher, coach, pastor, or family friend. Not only should we find a way to say thank you to those people, but we should also look for opportunities to repay their kindnesses to us by trying to make a difference in the lives of others. Our challenge in life is to seize upon every opportunity that comes our way to make a difference in the lives of others.

Point 4: Remember that Jesus did precisely this in each of our lives. His one life made a difference in the lives of untold generations who have put their faith in him. Humanity faced a great problem called sin. Jesus confronted that problem although it led him to death on the cross. None of the biblical characters who came before Christ had been willing or able to take on that challenge. It can truly be said that one life has made a difference for everyone who puts his or her faith and trust in Christ. Jesus was the "great person" whose life changed the course of history. In his name and following his example, we should all resolve at the start of this new year that, whether we earn headlines for our efforts or labor away in near obscurity, we will make sure that our lives make a difference.

Sermon Delivery

This text is a good candidate for some first-person or third-person preaching whereby a biblical narrative sets forth the thoughts and actions of David and then makes some appropriate application of that one life to all of our lives. This is a wonderful Scripture for this approach because it is so rich in dialogue, emotions, and physical activity, all of which can be presented quite vividly in a first- or third-person format.

Sermon Outcome

The desired outcome would be a heightened appreciation of the great people who have preceded us in history, the great people (including Jesus) who have changed our lives, and the greatness residing in each one of us if we have the faith and the courage to face a great problem, run a great risk, and do something that others before us could not or would not confront and resolve.

For Your Consideration

1. How is Martin Luther King Jr. Day observed in your church and community? Suggest additional ways in which your church might celebrate this day.

2. Who are the people whose lives have made a significant difference in your own life? Encourage listeners to consider this same question. Challenge them to find a way to thank those who have made a difference.

3. Ask people to think about how their lives have made a difference in the lives of others. Perhaps provide examples from the congregation of which you are aware.

4. Share how the life of Christ has made a measurable difference in *your* life.

The Story of Mary and Martha

For the Ordination of a Woman in Ministry

Text: Luke 10:38-42

Theme and Purpose

This sermon can be used to focus on the issue of women in ministry in particular and the so-called place and role of women in the church and in wider society more generally. There are four distinct points of view from which the sermon could be preached: the perspectives of Mary, Martha, Jesus, or one the twelve disciples. The sermon should be shaped so as to encourage women to embrace the example of Mary and thus move beyond the "place and role" that a male-dominated society has assigned to them.

Sermon Content

Point 1: Despite the way in which she had been socialized as a first-century-A.D. Jewish woman, Mary arrived at a day when she threw off her "place" in Jewish society and decided to move from the kitchen to the company of Jesus and his disciples. The text begins with the initial action taken by Mary. Nothing happens unless and until she makes the first move.

The ex-slave and abolitionist Frederick Douglass said, "Freedom is never granted by the oppressor; it must be demanded by the oppressed. Power yields nothing without demand." All people facing oppression and yearning for freedom can learn a lesson from Mary by taking the initiative to move away from the role they have been assigned and taking that first step into freedom.

Point 2: It is not only men who express opposition to women in ministry; other women are quite often opposed to the change in "role and place" as well. It was her own sister, Martha, not Jesus, who objected to what Mary had decided to do. Women pursuing careers in ministry have made this point over and over again. Whether it comes in the form of being reminded of what Paul said about women in ministry in 1 Corinthians 14:34-35 or 1 Timothy 2:12-14, or whether it comes in the form of some cruel comment or action, the church still hears the voices of men and women alike speaking against those women who are pursuing a call to ministry. There is always someone trying to pull people back into the limited role they have just thrown off.

Point 3: Say nothing to disparage the role that Martha plays in her home. The focus is not on Martha choosing to operate within the expected roles assigned to women at that time. Rather, the focus is on Mary's choice to redefine her place in her society. Some women may have something of both Mary and Martha at work within them. They may see themselves as servant leaders and wish to retain some of the Martha even as they pursue the Mary. This is fine, as long as women do not feel pressured (by others or by themselves) to accept this balancing act, one that by and large is not pressed upon their male counterparts. This text pushes us to be open to those women who tell us they do not want to be *limited* to the work that Martha performed with dignity and joy; some women want the option of sitting down and talking with Jesus as opposed to serving his meal.

Point 4: Jesus did not accept Martha's offer to rebuke Mary for assuming a new role in society. Instead, he applauded Mary for making the best choice. The importance of this point is that Jesus supports Mary not only in front of Martha, but also in front of his all-male disciples who might very well have objected to having Mary sitting among them. In neither case did Mary have to defend her decision to change roles, leaving the kitchen to sit with the men. Jesus was her defender. What can be better for a person taking the courageous step of seeking a new place in society than to know that when others seek to put you back in your place, Jesus will remind them and you that you have made the right choice?

Sermon Delivery

This sermon can be preached in a variety of ways. A first- or third-person sermon can choose from the perspective of any of the characters. Alternatively, you might opt for a thesis–antithesis–synthesis approach, as the sermon considers the steps necessary for women to achieve full equality in a society that still seeks to limit women to a "place" in our society.

Sermon Outcome

This sermon should motivate people to act on the issue of expanding the roles made available to women in our society. Women need to see that nothing will change *for* them unless and until something changes *within* them that causes them to follow Mary and move from the kitchen to the feet of Jesus. All women and men need to welcome and encourage those women who seek to take on new roles long denied them.

For Your Consideration

1. What biblical and theological teachings that inform your own views on the role of women in the ministry?
2. Discuss the experiences of any women you may know who are attempting to expand their role in the church by seeking ordination and a career in Christian ministry.
3. What gifts, experiences, and perspectives do women possess that might allow them, in some instances, to preach *more* effectively than their male counterparts?

Are You Righteous or Just Religious?

For a Church Anniversary
Text: Luke 10:25-37
Supporting Texts: Amos 5:24; Micah 6:8; Matt. 25:21

Theme and Purpose

This sermon is based on data compiled by the George Barna Research Institute that revealed something shocking about religious life in the United States—a significant discrepancy between a prevalent faith in God and a scant commitment to living out that faith. The purpose of the sermon is to challenge members of the congregation to narrow that gap between faith and practice.

Sermon Content

Introduction: According to a survey conducted by the George Barna Research institute, 94 percent of Americans claim to believe in the existence of God. Of that number, 45 percent said they attended some form of worship on a regular basis, with "regular" being defined as at least once a month. Of that second group of people, only 4 percent said they actually lived their daily lives according to the teachings of their religious affiliation. When 94 percent of the people believe in God, but only 4 percent of them practice their faith daily, there is ample reason to consider the difference between being *religious* and being *righteous*.

Point 1: The story of the Good Samaritan sets these two options in stark contrast. There is a man lying in the road who has been the victim of violence. You can see such people on streets and roads in a neighborhood near you. The question is not if we *see* the beaten man;

the question is whether or not we are willing to stop what we are doing and come to that man's aid. It is in such a moment that we discover whether we are religious or righteous.

Point 2: Three men were traveling along the road from Jerusalem to Jericho, and each one of them came upon the injured man. The first man to pass that way was a priest, a religious leader who must have been fully aware of the Mosaic laws dealing with showing love and mercy for those in distress (Micah 6:8; Amos 5:24). Nevertheless, the priest passed by on the other side of the road. A Levite also passed by, and this lay religious leader also looked at the beaten man and passed by on the other side.

The sign of religious persons is that they do things that leave people's deepest needs unmet by simply going through the motions of ritual and regulation. They say the right prayers at the right time and in the right way, but they do not address the deeper problems people are facing. For example, perhaps the priest in the parable was on his way to perform some religious ceremony, and if that beaten man were now dead, then the priest would have become ritually unclean and therefore unable to perform his "religious" functions. It was a good religious excuse! What kind of excuses do all but 4 percent of "believers" in America have?

Point 3: The work of righteousness was performed by the most unlikely person—a Samaritan. There was no greater oxymoron in ancient Jewish culture than a "good Samaritan." However, that was the person who did not pass by the beaten man lying on the road, leaving him in the same condition in which he'd found him. Instead, he displayed great love, mercy, and generosity on behalf of a fellow human being. He did what no law could require of him. It was compassion that moved his heart and ushered him into the ranks of the righteous.

The challenge faced by each one of us is to move *beyond* the ease and comfort of going to church on Sunday and to making sure we are among those who live out the words of Dr. Martin Luther King Jr., "If I can help somebody as I pass along, then my living will not be in vain."[3]

Sermon Delivery

This is a good text and topic on which to use the thesis –antithesis–synthesis approach. The thesis is that we should be righteous; the antithesis is that we are prevented from being truly righteous because we are not sufficiently committed to putting our faith into practice; and the synthesis is that God will accept nothing less than righteousness and will reward that quality in us by saying, "Well done, good and faithful servant" (Matthew 25:21, NIV).

Sermon Outcome

Based on the Barna research, it is evident that too few people actually practice what their religion teaches. This sermon should seek to energize people to make the move from religious rituals to acts of righteousness that touch and change the lives of those we meet on the roads of life.

For Your Consideration

1. Mention some of the actions and attitudes that you believe separate people who are truly righteous from those who are simply religious.

2. Are there any people or situations in your local community that need a helping hand? If so, has your church responded with religion or with righteousness?

3. Has a "good Samaritan" ever come into your life and displayed an unexpected form of kindness or compassion toward you? Consider using that experience as a sermon illustration.

4. Have you ever *been* a "good Samaritan" in the life of someone else, surprising them with a kindness they never expected from you?

The High Price of Popularity

For Holy Week
Text: Mark 15:1-15
Supporting Texts: Matt. 16:26; Rom. 7:19; Heb. 9:27

Theme and Purpose

This sermon is designed to focus on Pontius Pilate's decision to have Jesus crucified because he wanted to pacify the people. The price of Pilate's popularity with the people gathered in his courtyard that day was the death of Jesus, and that was a price Pilate was willing to pay. The purpose of this sermon is to encourage people never to place popularity with people over principles that are rooted in Scripture.

Sermon Content

Introduction: What reason can be given for Pilate sending Jesus to his death on the cross? What rationale or motivation led to Pilate's decision to inflict upon Jesus the most gruesome death conceived by the Roman authorities? If we consider this question by deduction, we can remove all the things that did not fuel his decision and be left with the only rationale the text can offer. There are four reasons built into the text that could and should have resulted in Pilate not condemning Jesus. There is only one reason offered by the text that explains his actions.

Point 1: The text tells us that Pilate repeatedly stated his belief in Jesus' innocence. The text reveals that Pilate *knew* those who clamored for the death of Jesus did so out of envy. The last thing Pilate wanted to do was approve a prisoner swap—Barabbas for Jesus—

because Barabbas had killed Roman soldiers in an attempted insurrection. Pilate could have called out the garrison of Roman soldiers under his command and ordered the courtyard to be cleared. Why didn't Pilate do any of these four things?

Point 2: The text declares the reason for Pilate's actions: he wanted to please the people in the courtyard. He had four good reasons *not* to do what he did, but he did it anyway. He condemned Jesus to the cross because he wanted to please the people. The sinless Son of God was condemned to death by crucifixion by a spineless governor who was willing to pay a very high price for popularity.

The philosopher George Savile said, "Popularity is a crime the minute you start seeking after it." If a person can gain and retain popularity without having to compromise or ignore his or her deeply held personal convictions, there is no danger. However, if the only way to gain popularity with some person or group is to lower one's moral standards, then the price of popularity may be too high. As Jesus said in Matthew 16:26, "What will it profit them if they gain the whole world but forfeit their life?"

Point 3: Each one of us has known a moment like the one faced by Pilate, a time when we knew the right thing to do but did not do it because we did not want to risk our popularity with or acceptance by some person or group. In Romans 7:19, Paul wrote, "For I do not do the good I want, but the evil I do not want is what I do." We cannot point fingers at Pilate, because on more than one occasion, we also may have lowered our standards or looked the other way or did what we knew was wrong just to gain or maintain popularity with someone.

The only solution to this is to remember Hebrews 9:27: "It is appointed for mortals to die once, and after that the judgment." We need to pursue approval from and popularity with God, and not risk that in order to gain the approval of people. More than we should want to hear other people tell us how "cool" or "in" or "wonderful" we are, we ought to live so as to hear God say, "Well done."

Sermon Delivery

This could be a sermon based on deduction in which you eliminate one by one the options Pilate had before him (and the reasons he might have chosen one of them), finally settling on the choice he made and the tragic reason he made this choice: he wanted to please the people.

Sermon Outcome

This sermon should challenge people to place values and principles over popularity and public pressure. We all face choices similar to those of Pontius Pilate in that we are tempted to do what we already know is wrong. Hopefully, this sermon will encourage people to please God and not others when these moments come.

For Your Consideration

1. Share a decision you have made in your life that was more influenced by your desire to be popular with a group than it was on being pleasing to God.

2. Ask people to consider whether there are any groups or individuals they are so intent on pleasing that they would compromise on a matter of moral or ethical principle. Perhaps list a few possibilities.

3. Explore what you think Pilate should have done with Jesus. Would you have done things differently if you were in the exact same circumstance? Why or why not?

4. Cite examples of contemporary public officials (or people from history) who have exhibited the same trait as Pontius Pilate. Conversely, cite examples of leaders who acted differently from Pilate, who did what they felt was right regardless of the cost in popularity.

The Greatest Gift Ever Given

For Christmas

Text: John 3:16

Supporting Texts: Prov. 18:24; Isa. 7:14; Matt. 1:23; Rom. 5:8

Theme and Purpose

This sermon is designed to set in tension two Christmas holiday songs: "Santa Claus Is Coming to Town" and "Joy to the World." These two songs point to the very different ways in which Christmas is observed throughout the country. For most people Christmas is all about the gifts we give to and hope to receive from others. The focus should be on the unmerited gift all of us have already received from God in the form of salvation through Jesus Christ.

Sermon Content

Introduction: With every passing year it seems that Christmas is less and less about Christ and more and more about Santa Claus. It is less about God's unmerited love and favor and more about Santa's unlimited supply of gifts and goodies for those who have been "nice" and not "naughty" during the year. Christmas has become more of a shopping season and less of a spiritual observance. Department stores begin decorating even before Thanksgiving Day has arrived. Christmas really begins with the busiest shopping day of the year, the day after Thanksgiving, a full month before Christmas. The challenge that confronts the church in general, and each individual Christian in particular, is to remind ourselves and our world that Christmas is about the Savior and not the Santa.

Point 1: Built into the song "Santa Claus Is Coming to Town"[4] are the things that separate Jesus Christ from this mythical figure from the North Pole whose bearded face and reindeer-driven sleigh seem to dominate the holiday landscape. The song says that Santa Claus "is coming to town." The implication is that except for that one day of the year when he makes his rounds to deliver his gifts, Santa Claus is not with us or available to us. He comes and he goes.

Point 2: The second aspect of Santa's gift-giving policy turns on the phrase, "He's gonna find out who's naughty or nice." The song goes on to say, "He knows if you've been bad or good, so be good for goodness' sake." In the Gospel according to Santa Claus, gifts are given only on one day each year and only to those who have been "nice" or "good." For all the other days of the year and for all those persons who do not fall within the "nice" and the "good" category, Santa Claus has nothing to offer.

Point 3: In the Gospel according to Jesus Christ, the message is very different. The difference begins with the idea of giving gifts. The focus is not on the expensive and elaborate gifts we give and receive among ourselves. Instead, the gift is the precious and priceless gift of Christ himself and the salvation that came with him when he entered into the world. Hear John 3:16 tell us: "For God so loved the world that he gave his only Son." This is truly the greatest gift ever given. There is a haunting Christmas song that raises this question: "Mary, did you know . . . that the child that you delivered will soon deliver you?"[5] That is the true gift of the Christmas season.

Point 4: Jesus differs from Santa Claus in another significant way. While Santa's gifts are reserved for the "nice" and the "good," the gift of salvation through Jesus Christ is available to "whosoever" is willing to believe. In Romans 5:8 Paul wrote, "While we were still sinners Christ died for us." The work of salvation was not put on hold until we straightened out our lives and got back on track with God. Instead, as the familiar song says, "He looked beyond my faults and saw my needs."[6]

It is sad, but probably safe to say that most of us fill out a Christmas shopping list that reflects the values of Santa Claus far more than they reflect the values of Jesus Christ. We give only to those who have been "nice" and "good" to us. We do not offer anything to people who have been rude or mean-spirited or unkind. We want Jesus to look beyond our faults and see our needs, but we seldom if ever do the same for one another.

Point 5: There is a third difference between Jesus Christ and Santa Claus, and this involves the length of their stay among us. Santa Claus comes to town and then leaves for a year, not to be seen or heard from until the next Christmas rolls around. By contrast, our relationship with Jesus has everlasting ties. In Matthew 1:23 we are told, "'They shall name him Emmanuel, which means 'God with us'" (see also Isaiah 7:14). The very name given to Jesus points to this difference between the "right jolly old elf" and the babe of Bethlehem. We can pray to him every day of the year. We can lean on him every day of the year. We can count on him every day of the year. And when life gives way to death and we can't take with us the gifts and goodies Santa has brought, the Lord Jesus Christ will be there to usher us into his kingdom and his eternal presence. That gift is a great deal better than anything offered by Santa Claus.

Point 6: The time has surely come when Christians should exert every effort to rescue Christmas from the culture that invites people to give a Lexus automobile or a Rolex watch as a holiday gift, completely ignoring the fact that the Person behind the holiday was born into poverty in a manger in Bethlehem. My slave ancestors were right in their theology when they sang, "You can have all this world, just give me Jesus."7 Let those who choose to observe Christmas according to the gospel of Santa Claus be reminded of what they are missing—a priceless gift from God, love and grace that is not dependent on our goodness, and a "friend who sticks closer than a brother" (Proverbs 18:24).

Point 7: Turn aside from the superficial cheer to be found in a foolish song like "Santa Claus Is Coming to Town," and exchange it for true joy in the great hymn of the church, "Joy to the World"![8] That hymn, which is set to the music of Beethoven's "Ode to Joy," celebrates the entire package—Christmas in verses 1 and 2, the victory over sin in verse 3, and the kingdom of God in verse 4. That's the gift that keeps on giving all year round. It is the only gift worth celebrating year after year after year.

Sermon Delivery
This sermon is ideally suited for the dialectic approach of thesis/antithesis/synthesis. Points 1 and 2 set up the thesis, which is Santa. Points 3, 4, and 5 establish how Jesus is the antithesis to old St. Nick. And Points 6 and 7 neatly synthesize the entire argument—that Jesus is superior to Santa in every way.

Sermon Outcome
This sermon draws a sharp contrast between the two ways in which Christmas is celebrated in our country, and having done so, challenges people to choose the approach that has the most lasting value. All four sermon outcomes can be used in this sermon. The

introduction can kindle the mind, points 1–2 can disturb the conscience, points 3–5 can stir the heart, and points 6–7 can energize the will to take action.

For Your Consideration

1. List some things your church can do to keep the focus of Christmas on the gift that God has given us in Jesus Christ and not on the gifts we give to one another.

2. Ask the people to think about their Christmas lists. Do their lists include only those persons they like and who have been "nice" to them during the year?

3. Share some examples of things you have seen locally that illustrate how our culture has come to associate Christmas merely with giving or receiving gifts.

The Power and Purpose of Pentecost

For Pentecost Sunday
Text: Acts 1:6-8; 2:1-12
Suggested Texts: Matt. 28:18-20; Acts 1:4-5; 2:17

Theme and Purpose

This sermon is intended to remind faithful Christians that Pentecost is an observance of comparable value with Christmas and Easter and should be celebrated every year with equal joy and reverence. Most churches have elaborate pageants, decorations, and festivities to mark Christmas and Easter, but they tend to skip over Pentecost without a word. This sermon provides reasons Pentecost should be observed.

Sermon Content

Introduction: How would you feel if your birthday came and went year after year and nobody sent you a card or sang "Happy Birthday" or acknowledged your special day in any way? Most of us keep close track of our birthdays, and if nobody else buys us a gift, we are certain to buy something for ourselves. The observance of birthdays is a very important thing.

Point 1: How strange it is that people who value birthday parties for themselves seem completely unaware of the day when Christians are called upon annually to acknowledge and celebrate the birthday of the Christian church. Pentecost is the observance when we are called upon to remember the day in Jerusalem when there was the promised outpouring of the Holy Spirit, the speaking in tongues among the disciples, the bold and forceful sermon of the previously frightened and unfaithful Peter, and the three thousand souls who were converted on a single afternoon. Pentecost marks the first day in the life of the Christian church.

Maybe you assumed that Pentecost is celebrated only by people of Pentecostal denominations—Assemblies of God, Church of God in Christ, among others. Nothing could be further from the truth. Pentecost is no more to be observed only by Pentecostals than baptism is to be observed only by Baptists. It is a day to be observed by all Christians; it is the birthday party for the church to which all believers are invited, regardless of denominational labels or worship styles. After all, it was Jesus himself who issued the first invitation to this Holy Spirit party (Acts 1:4-5).

Point 2: Pentecost carries some significant theological themes that will go unaddressed unless this day is carefully observed. Pentecost marks the day when the responsibility for spreading the message of the gospel was assigned to the disciples. Prior to that time, all of the work had been done by God through Christ. It was God at work in Christ who accomplished the work of incarnation in Bethlehem. It was God at work in Christ who accomplished the work of atonement and reconciliation on the cross. It was God at work in Christ who accomplished the victory of life over death, hell, and the grave.

All of this work was done *for* us, but not *by* us. Pentecost marks the point in the gospel story when we stop being recipients and beneficiaries and start becoming workers and witnesses who carry the message of the gospel to the ends of the earth.

Point 3: Pentecost reminds us that while the work has been assigned to us, we will need the power of the Holy Spirit to accomplish that work. Remember: Jesus commissioned the disciples in Matthew 28:18-20, but they weren't fully empowered to *do* the work until the day of Pentecost when the Holy Spirit was poured out on them. The power is not ours; it comes from God. Churches are not built solely by visions and long-range planning, or by fund-raising projects and tithing programs. Churches are built as the Holy Spirit works through us and, sometimes, despite us.

Point 4: Pentecost reminds us every year that racism, chauvinism, sexism, and other prejudices have a way of deciding the composition of the congregation with whom we worship the Lord, who created all people to live together on the face of the earth. Pentecost offers an annual critique of how deeply divided by race and ethnicity our churches are to this day—in stark contrast with the crowd that gathered in Jerusalem to hear Peter's sermon. The three thousand who were added to the church that day came from every nation and region of the known world. They came from Africa, Europe, Asia, the Mediterranean region, the deserts of Arabia, and even the Persian Gulf. They were a multiethnic crowd who were transformed into a congregation of believers when they heard the gospel.

Pentecost also reminds us that since God can pour

his Holy Spirit upon our sons *and* our daughters (Acts 2:17), we need to consider where women fit in the life of our congregations and denominations. In short, Pentecost is a day we should not overlook. It is a birthday party we dare not miss, no matter who we look like, what language we speak, or what denomination receives our tithe.

Sermon Delivery

Doctrinal sermons such as this one usually have a didactic or instructional form. Many forms could be used in this case, including the expository approach of "tell them, tell them, and tell them." Storytelling can also work well because there is so much drama to narrate. This outline uses more of an inductive method to make its point: If we have time for and interest in Christmas and Easter, then we need to make similar time for and show equal interest in Pentecost.

Sermon Outcome

This sermon is designed to accomplish the goals suggested by the four major points of the sermon: highlight the importance of observing the day of Pentecost, embrace the work that is assigned to the church at Pentecost, understand that the work that is ours can be accomplished only by the power that comes from God, and encourage people to value (and, hopefully, reflect) the diversity that was present in the crowd when Peter preached his first sermon on the Day of Pentecost.

For Your Consideration
1. How does your church or other churches you know of observe (or fail to observe) Pentecost Sunday? Suggest some ways that you must initiate a celebration of Pentecost in your congregation or community.

2. How are the power and presence of the Holy Spirit evident in the life of your congregation? How might that power and presence be amplified?

3. Does your congregation have the diversity that was present in the crowd on the first Day of Pentecost? Would you preach a sermon that challenged your congregation to be open to more diversity both in your membership and in your leadership?

Help Wanted!
To Call Christians into Active Ministry
Text: Exod. 17:8-13; Mark 2:1-5
Supporting Texts: Matt. 9:37-38; Rom. 12:4-8; 1 Cor. 12:12-26; Eph. 4:11-14

Theme and Purpose
This sermon is designed to move the congregation beyond attendance at worship services and toward taking on an active role in the life of the church and in

the work of the kingdom of God. The central challenge is to remind Christians that the pastor and ordained clergy are not the only persons who should be doing the work of the ministry. Like Aaron and Hur, who held up the arms of Moses, and like the four anonymous men who carried a paralytic man to Jesus, the work of the church can be accomplished only when everyone plays a part.

Sermon Content

Introduction: People are familiar with the idea of "Help Wanted" when it comes to a company or a store advertising to fill a vacancy in its workforce. "Help Wanted" ads can be seen in the newspaper, in store windows, and on electric signs in front of factories or manufacturing plants. God also sends out "want ads" for service in the life of the church. This sermon is a "Help Wanted" message designed to encourage people to answer the call to Christian service.

Point 1: Begin with the story of Moses in the battle against the Amalekites and the essential role played by Aaron and Hur in allowing Israel to prevail and be preserved as a nation. Moses was clearly the leader of the people of Israel, but in one instance after another, it is clear that he did not and could not have done his job without help from other people. In this text, as long as Moses held up the staff of God in his hands, the army fighting under the leadership of Joshua prevailed in the battle. However, when his arms grew weary and the staff lowered, the army would begin to lose. Not only did Moses need Joshua to lead the fight against the Amalekites, but he also needed Aaron and Hur to hold up his arms when he no longer had the strength to do so on his own.

In every church there is a need for people beyond the pastor and other leaders to be involved. That's why Ephesians 4:11-14 establishes that the work of pastors and teachers is to equip all the saints for the work of the ministry. That work requires *every* member to play a part. Indeed, Romans 12:4-8 reminds us that not only does every member of the body of Christ have a gift he or she can use in the service of God, but each of us also has a responsibility to use that gift. Too many churchgoers, it seems, think that their sole duty is to hear the sermon and go home. No wonder Jesus said in Matthew 9:37-38: "The harvest is plentiful but the laborers are few."

Someone once described a football game as twenty-two players who badly need some rest being observed by thousands of spectators who badly need some exercise. Many churches are just like that, with a few people doing all the work while others simply observe from the sidelines. Christianity is not a spectator sport!

Point 2: Aaron and Hur did not attempt to remove the staff from the hand of Moses, and they did not try to replace Joshua on the field of battle. They saw their role as being equally important, even if it may have appeared to be less glamorous. Playing a supporting role in a Hollywood film can provide as much of a chance for an actor to win an Oscar as playing the lead. There is a song that says, "If I can help somebody as I pass along, then my living will not be in vain."[9] That's the essence of Paul's message in 1 Corinthians 12:12-26, where he observes that each believer is a part of Christ's body, and no part is less vital than any other. We are each an indispensable part of the whole. Help is wanted, especially in support roles where there is little in the way of worldly recognition, but about which God will surely say, "Well done."

Point 3: In the passage in Mark 2, a paralytic is brought before Jesus by the combined efforts of four men. And these men did not offer a half-hearted try at being helpful; they went above and beyond the call of duty by lifting the paralyzed man up onto a roof and then lowering him through a hole into the presence of Jesus. They joined their compassion with their conviction and got the job done. They received no accolades for their efforts; their names are never mentioned. All they got for their help was a miracle from Jesus, who was so impressed by their faith that he healed their paralyzed friend. The work we are called upon to do may sometimes be difficult and challenging, but if the end result is that we can bring someone to wholeness and healing from Christ, then it was well worth the effort.

On a typical sports team at any level, some players may get more notoriety, but all players are important. The quarterback may have the highest profile, but the center has to snap the ball, the running backs have to get the handoff, the receivers have to catch the pass, and all the other players have to block in order for the play to be successful. Similarly, in the above account from the New Testament, the combined and dedicated efforts of all four men were needed to get the paralyzed man to Jesus. It is likely that anything less than all four men working together would not have been enough.

Point 4: From Exodus 17, we know it was Aaron and Hur who helped Moses. At least their names were called. In Mark 2, all we read is, "Some men came bringing him a paralytic, who was carried by four of them" (NIV). No names were given by Mark, and no names were asked for by Jesus. The focus was not on them; the focus was entirely on the man they were trying to help. Can you imagine a church where no plaques were given, no certificates of recognition offered, and no names placed in the weekly bulletin? Very few people would be willing to work under such conditions. We want the world to know everything we have done. But the affirmation that should be most important to us comes from Jesus and not from one another.

Sermon Delivery

Here is a good place for the argument of induction, or an a priori approach, proceeding as follows: If Aaron and Hur were willing to help Moses and if four anonymous men were willing to help the paralytic man, then we as Christians should also look for ways that we can be helpful in the life of our church and in the work of God's kingdom.

Sermon Outcome

From beginning to end, this sermon should challenge and motivate listeners to find an area of ministry in the life of their church and to lend a hand. In particular, the goal is to introduce people to areas of ministry in which they can be involved without consideration of whether or not they will ever receive any credit or recognition for their efforts. The emphasis should be on the help we extend and not the attention we receive.

For Your Consideration

1. Include in your yearly preaching schedule at least one sermon designed to encourage people to become

more active in a hands-on way in the ministries of your local church.

2. When in your life have you been called on to play a *supporting* role? Your congregation would benefit from hearing about that experience from someone they view exclusively as a leading actor.

3. When in your ministry have you felt the support of others who have walked alongside you in ministry?

4. List some of the areas in your church's ministry where there are opportunities for people to contribute. Consider making this sermon part of a larger recruitment campaign to involve members more extensively.

What Things Last Forever?

For Reformation Sunday
Text: Isa. 40:6-8; Matt. 16:13-20
Supporting Texts: Matt. 6:19-21; Heb. 13:8

Theme and Purpose

This sermon is intended to remind the Christian community of God's promise that the Word of God (the Bible), the people of God, the church, and the presence of Jesus Christ will last even when everything else around us withers and fades away. All human institutions and all human achievements will at some point go out of style, then fall out of use or usefulness, and finally pass out of existence. But this is not the case for these three things God has given us: the authority of Scripture, the ministry of the church, and the active presence of Christ until the end of time.

Sermon Content

Introduction: There was a time when Sears & Roebuck was the dominant retail company in the world, and a chain of stores now known as Wal-Mart did not exist. The world has changed, and many of the stores and companies with which we grew up have downsized, are in bankruptcy court, or are out of business altogether. There was a time when a major league baseball team called the Dodgers played in Brooklyn, New York, but they have long since moved to Los Angeles. There was a time when the National Football League team known as the Rams played in Los Angeles, but now they play in St. Louis. There was a time when the National Basketball Association team known as the Jazz played (not surprisingly, in New Orleans) but that was before they moved to Salt Lake City, Utah.

In the world of sports, as in the world of business, things are constantly changing. Is there anything that does *not* change? Are there things that do *not* relocate or go out of business? Are there any things that last forever? There are at least three things that meet the criteria of "lasting forever," despite how much the world around them may change: the Bible, the Christian church, and Jesus Christ himself.

Point 1: Isaiah 40:6-8 reminds us that the "word of God" will stand forever. This means that the teachings of God, the promises of God, and the intentions of God for creation as spelled out in Scripture will remain in force long after nations and kingdoms rise and fall. It is important to remember that while America is busy debating what role it wants God to have in our secular, multicultural society, the Word of God will still be read and revered long after America has followed every other great nation or empire into the dust of the earth and into the annals of history. "The grass withers and the flowers fade, but the word of our God will last forever" (Isaiah 40:8).

There are nearly one million books in the main library at Harvard University, one of the largest libraries in the world. The vast majority of them are preserved on microfilm because they are no longer being widely read. Most of the books in that great library are out of circulation. That is not the case with the Bible. It remains the best-selling book of all time. It is regularly being reprinted not only in English, but in virtually every known language on earth. Talk about having the last word!

Point 2: The nation of Israel would never be the same again. Isaiah 40 is set at the end of the exile in Babylon, and from that point on Israel would be little more than a pawn in the political chess game that involved first Persia, then Greece, and finally Rome. However, the teachings by which God's people should govern their lives—no matter where on earth they lived—would never change. A Jew was no longer necessarily a person who lived in Judea or Galilee. A Jew was a person who lived according to the law of God, which had not changed. Similarly, a Christian is not simply a person who attends a church on Sunday morning. A Christian is someone who lives every day of his or her life in obedience to the teachings of God and the example of Jesus.

Point 3: Not only will the Bible last forever, but in Matthew 16 Jesus told his disciples that he was going to establish his church upon the faith and testimony of Peter—and "the gates of hell will not prevail against it." If hell itself cannot destroy the church, then it seems safe to say that the church of Jesus Christ is something else that will last forever.

The historic Pilgrim Baptist Church of Chicago, where Thomas A. Dorsey and Mahalia Jackson defined and perfected gospel music in the 1930s and 1940s, was destroyed by a fire early in 2006. Dorsey's manuscripts were burned up, but his music, his melodies, and his message in songs such as "Precious Lord, Take My Hand" were sung in churches across this country the very next Sunday.

You see, the church Jesus was talking about was not a particular building nor even a particular denomination. Those structures and institutions didn't exist then. Church buildings, individual congregations, even denominational groups may rise and fall, but the church as the witnessing community of believers in Jesus Christ will last forever, or at least until the end of time when Christ returns.

In a 1998 survey the George Barna Research Institute observed that unless the churches of America become more relevant to the needs of people, there is a chance that the Christian faith could become extinct—deemed irrelevant and ineffective—in this country.

In a separate survey, Barna documented that the Christian faith has already become virtually extinct in Europe, with the vast majority expressing no faith in God and no active membership in any Christian denomination. While Barna's warnings should not be ignored, our hope is not in George Barna, but in Jesus Christ and his promise that his church will stand until he comes at the end time to gather the church unto himself. We must cling to that promise even if only a "remnant" of believers remains.

Point 4: In the Sermon on the Mount in Matthew 6:19-21, Jesus warned the people not to establish their lives on things that "moth and rust can consume or that robbers can break in and steal." Rather, we should establish our lives on things that last forever and do not diminish with the passing of years. God's Word qualifies; the church of Jesus Christ qualifies; and according to Hebrews 13:8, Jesus himself also qualifies: "Jesus Christ is the same yesterday, today, and forever."

The third everlasting component of our faith is Jesus Christ himself. Not only does the Word of God, which is the Bible, last forever, but the Word of God that is Jesus Christ will also last forever! He was dead, but now he is alive forevermore. As Protestants, the offspring of the Reformation, this is no small point. Martin Luther's disagreement with Pope Leo X in 1519 was over the matter of authority. For Luther, authority was not in the office of the pope; authority was in Christ and in the Bible. Dozens of popes have lived and died since 1519. Pope Benedict XVI is the sixth pope to reign since I was born in 1948. However, Jesus Christ is as he has always been and always will be—the same yesterday, today, and forever.

Sermon Delivery

This message could take on a variety of voices. It could be delivered as a challenge to renewed commitment to study God's Word. It could be an exhortation to cast off apathy in the church. It could be encouragement in a season of grief, loss, or despair, when things of this life seem to be slipping through mortal fingers. It could also be doctrinal in orientation, establishing the historical context of the Protestant Reformation and your denomination's place in that tradition.

Sermon Outcome

No matter what approach you take to this topic and the texts, the outcome is essentially the same. The congregation should be left with a bedrock certainty that there are three things in this life that they can stand on: the Word of God, the church of God, and the Son of God, Jesus Christ. That bedrock certainty can be an anchor in the storm, a foundation to build on, or a launchpad inspiring a countdown to revival!

For Your Consideration

1. Illustrate your sermon with mention of former corporations, factories, department stores, or other businesses that once thrived in your community or region but are now out of business.

2. Highlight and discuss any signs of renewal in the life of the church in your community. What new churches are being planted? Which established churches are showing signs of growth and revival?

3. What specific steps can you take as a church to prevent the fulfillment of George Barna's predictions concerning the possible extinction of the Christian faith in America?

Notes

1. "Amazing Grace," words by John Newton, 1779, public domain.

2. "In Lovingkindness Jesus Came," words and music by Charles H. Gabriel, 1905, public domain.

3. "If I Can Help Somebody," words by Alma Hazel Androzzo, © 1958 Boosey and Hawkes Inc. ASCAP. These lyrics were immortalized by Martin Luther King Jr. in his sermon "The Drum Major Instinct," delivered at Ebenezer Baptist Church, Atlanta, Georgia, February 1968.

4. "Santa Claus Is Coming to Town," words and music by J. Fred Coots and Haven Gillespie, 1934.

5. "Mary, Did You Know?" by Mark Lowry and Buddy Greene, © 1991 by Word Music/Rufus Music/ASCAP.

6. "He Looked beyond My Faults," words by Dottie Rambo, copyright by Brentwood Benson Music Publishing.

7. "Give Me Jesus," traditional Negro spiritual, public domain.

8. "Joy to the World," words by Isaac Watts, 1719, public domain.

9. "If I Can Help Somebody," Androzzo.

Recommended Reading

Many, many books dealing with various aspects of preaching, exegesis, hermeneutics, and communication in the postmodern era are available—so many in fact that preachers might benefit from some guidance as to which books they may want to consult and, perhaps, to purchase. The following suggestions are grouped by category. While every book listed in each category is useful, preachers would be wise to acquire at least a few from each grouping.

Preaching and Exegesis: These books assist with the initial task of textual analysis as a preparation for sermon design.

Allen, Ronald J. *Contemporary Biblical Interpretation for Preaching.* Valley Forge, PA: Judson Press, 1984.

Long, Thomas G. *Preaching and the Literary Forms of the Bible.* Philadelphia: Fortress Press, 1989.

—— *The Witness of Preaching.* Louisville: Westminster/John Knox Press, 2005.

McMickle, Marvin A. *Living Water for Thirsty Souls.* Valley Forge, PA: Judson Press, 2001.

Thompson, William. *Preaching Biblically: Exegesis and Interpretation.* Nashville: Abingdon, 1981.

Wilder, Amos. *Early Christian Rhetoric: The Language of the Gospel.* Cambridge, MA: Harvard University Press, 1971.

Preaching and the Bible: These books provide insight on how to approach preaching from various books and genres of the Bible.

Achtemeier, Elizabeth. *Preaching from the Old Testament*. Louisville: Westminster/John Knox Press, 1989.

Blomberg, Craig L. *Preaching the Parables*. Grand Rapids: Baker, 2003.

Braxton, Brad. *Preaching Paul*. Nashville: Abingdon, 2004.

Bryson, Harold T. *Expository Preaching*. Nashville: Broadman and Holman, 1995.

Dodd, C. H. *The Parables of the Kingdom*. New York: Scribner & Sons, 1961.

Greidanus, Sidney. *The Modern Preacher and the Ancient Text*. Grand Rapids: Eerdmans, 1990.

———. *Preaching Christ from the Old Testament*. Grand Rapids: Eerdmans, 1999.

MacArthur, John Jr. *Expository Preaching*. Dallas: Word, 1992.

Mathewson, Steven D. *The Art of Preaching Old Testament Narratives*. Grand Rapids: Baker, 2002.

Stiller, Brian. *Preaching Parables to Postmoderns*. Philadelphia: Fortress Press, 2004.

Ward, James, and Christine Ward. *Preaching from the Prophets*. Nashville: Abingdon, 1995.

Sermon Construction and Design: Collectively, these books provide more than a hundred years of insight into the art of how to structure a sermon.

Broadus, John. *On the Preparation and Delivery of Sermons*. 1872. Reprint, New York: Harper and Row, 1944.

Buttrick, David. *Homiletic: Moves and Structures*. Philadelphia: Fortress Press, 1987.

Craddock, Fred. *As One without Authority*. St. Louis: Chalice Press, 2001.

———. *Preaching*. Nashville: Abingdon, 1985.

Davis, H. Grady. *Design for Preaching*. Philadelphia: Fortress Press, 1958.

Jones, Ilion T. *Principles and Practices of Preaching*. Nashville: Abingdon, 1956.

Massey, James Earl. *Designing the Sermon*. Nashville: Abingdon, 1980.

Proctor, Samuel D. *The Certain Sound of the Trumpet: Crafting a Sermon of Authority*. Valley Forge, PA: Judson Press, 1994.

Richard, Ramesh. *Preparing Evangelistic Sermons: A Seven-Step Method for Preaching Salvation*. Grand Rapids: Baker, 2005.

Robinson, Haddon. *Biblical Preaching*. Grand Rapids: Baker, 1980.

———, ed. *Biblical Sermons*. Grand Rapids: Baker, 1989.

———, and Craig B. Larson, eds. *The Art and Craft of Biblical Preaching*. Grand Rapids: Zondervan, 2004.

Sangster, W. E. *The Craft of the Sermon*. Philadelphia: Westminster Press, 1951.

History of Preaching: These books offer insights into the origins and development of preaching, dating back to the early Christian community.

Brilioth, Yngve. *A Brief History of Preaching.* Philadelphia: Fortress Press, 1945.

Dargan, Edwin Charles. *A History of Preaching, Volume One: A.D. 70–1572.* Reprint, Grand Rapids: Baker, 1954.

———. *A History of Preaching, Volume Two: 1572–1900.* New York: Hodden-Stoughton Press, 1912.

Dodd, C. H. *The Apostolic Preaching.* New York: Harper and Row, 1964.

Edwards, O. C. *A History of Preaching.* Nashville: Abingdon, 2004.

Fant, Clyde E. Jr., and William M. Pinson Jr., *Twenty Centuries of Great Preaching: 10 Volumes.* Waco, TX: Word, 1971.

Holland, DeWitte. *Preaching in American History: 1630–1967.* Nashville: Abingdon, 1969.

———. *The Preaching Tradition: A Brief History.* Nashville: Abingdon, 1980.

———. *Sermons in American History: 1630–1967.* Nashville: Abingdon, 1971.

Willimon, William H., and Richard Lischer, eds. *Concise Encyclopedia of Preaching.* Louisville: Westminster/John Knox Press, 1995.

Preaching and Oral Communication: These books discuss the skills and techniques that contribute to the development of clear and effective preaching.

Chartier, Myron. *Preaching as Communication*. Nashville: Abingdon, 1981.

Childers, Jana. *Performing the Word: Preaching as Theatre*. Nashville: Abingdon, 1998.

Duduit, Michael, ed. *Communicating with Power: Insights from America's Top Communicators*. Grand Rapids: Baker, 1996.

Fasol, Al. *A Complete Guide to Sermon Delivery*. Nashville: Broadman and Holman, 1996.

———. *A Guide to Self-Improvement in Sermon Delivery*. Grand Rapids: Baker, 1983.

Jones, Edgar DeWitt, ed. *Masters of Speech: Portraits of Fifteen American Orators*. Grand Rapids: Baker, 1975.

Koller, Charles W. *Expository Preaching without Notes and Sermons Preached without Notes*. Grand Rapids: Baker, 1962.

Nichols, J. Randall. *Building the Word: The Dynamics of Communicating and Preaching*. New York: Harper and Row, 1980.

Sermon Anthologies: These books are collections of sermons that offer a wide sampling of styles, topics, cultures, and historical contexts.

Fasol, Al, ed. *Selected Readings in Preaching: Classic Contributions from Pulpit Masters*. Grand Rapids: Baker, 1979.

Lischer, Richard, ed. *The Company of Preachers: Wisdom on Preaching from Augustine to the Present*. Grand Rapids: Eerdmans, 2002.

Long, Thomas G., and Cornelius Plantinga Jr., eds. *A Chorus of Witnesses: Model Sermons for Today's Preachers*. Grand Rapids: Eerdmans, 1994.

Roberts, Richard O., ed. *Salvation in Full Color: Twenty Sermons by Great Awakening Preachers*. Wheaton, IL: International Awakening Press, 1994.

Thornton, John F., and Katherine Washburn, eds. *Tongues of Angels/Tongues of Men: A Book of Sermons*. New York: Doubleday, 1999.

Warner, Michael, ed. *American Sermons: The Pilgrims to Martin Luther King Jr.* N.p.: Library of America, 1999.

Wiersbe, Warren, ed. *Treasury of the World's Greatest Sermons*. Grand Rapids: Kregel, 1993.

Theory and Theology of Preaching: These books offer insights into the biblical and theological rationales for preaching, as well as observations from various scholars about their views of the preaching task.

Gibson, Scott, ed. *Preaching to a Shifting Culture*. Grand Rapids: Baker, 2004.

Gonzalez, Justo, and Pablo Jiminez. *Pulpito: An Introduction to Hispanic Preaching*. Nashville: Abingdon, 2005.

Graves, Mike, ed. *What's the Matter with Preaching Today?* Louisville: Westminster/John Knox Press, 2004.

Johnston, Graham. *Preaching to a Post-Modern World*. Grand Rapids: Baker, 2001.

Jones, Kirk Byron. *The Jazz of Preaching: How to Preach with Great Freedom and Joy*. Nashville: Abingdon, 2004.

Lischer, Richard. *A Theology of Preaching*. Nashville: Abingdon, 1981.

Lowry, Eugene L. *The Homiletical Plot*. Atlanta: John Knox Press, 1980.

———. *Living with the Lectionary*. Nashville: Abingdon, 1992.

Massey, James Earl. *The Burdensome Joy of Preaching*. Nashville: Abingdon, 1998.

McKim, Donald K. *The Bible in Theology and Preaching*. Eugene, OR: Wipf and Stock, 1999.

Mitchell, Henry H. *Celebration and Experience in Preaching*. Nashville: Abingdon, 1990.

———. *The Recovery of Preaching*. New York: Harper and Row, 1977.

Mohler, R. Albert, et al. *Feed My Sheep: A Passionate Plea for Preaching*. Morgan, PA: Soli Deo Gloria Publications, 2002.

Willimon, William. *Proclamation and Theology*. Nashville: Abingdon, 2005.

Preaching in the African American Tradition: These books deal with the sociocultural distinctives of black preaching, as well as the diversity of forms and voices from within the black church community.

Bond, Susan L. *Contemporary African American Preaching: Diversity in Theory and Style*. St. Louis: Chalice Press, 2003.

Blount, Brian K. *Go Preach! Mark's Kingdom Message*

and the Black Church Today. Maryknoll, NY: Orbis, 1998.

Crawford, Evans E. *The Hum: Call and Response in African American Preaching*. Nashville: Abingdon, 1995.

Furlow, Clayton D. *A Theology of Preaching in the African-American Context*. Lithonia, GA: Orman Press, 2004.

Harris, James H. *Preaching Liberation*. Philadelphia: Fortress Press, 1996.

———. *The Word Made Plain*. Minneapolis: Fortress, 2004.

Hoard, Walter B., ed. *Outstanding Black Sermons: Volume 2*. Reprint, Valley Forge, PA: Judson Press, 2000.

LaRue, Cleophus. *The Heart of Black Preaching*. Louisville: Westminster/John Knox Press, 2000.

———, ed. *Power in the Pulpit: How America's Most Effective Black Preachers Prepare Their Sermons*. Louisville: Westminster/John Knox Press, 2002.

McMickle, Marvin A. *Preaching to the Black Middle Class: Words of Challenge, Words of Hope*. Valley Forge, PA: Judson Press, 2000.

Mitchell, Henry H. *Black Preaching*. Nashville: Abingdon, 1990.

———, and Emil M. Thomas. *Preaching for Black Self-Esteem*. Nashville: Abingdon, 1994.

Moyd, Olin P. *The Sacred Art: Preaching and Theology in the African American Tradition*. Valley Forge, PA: Judson Press, 1995.

Myers, William H. *The Irresistible Urge to Preach: African American Call Stories*. Atlanta: Aaron Press, 1992.

Newbold, Robert, ed. *Black Preaching: Select Sermons in the Presbyterian Tradition*. Philadelphia: The Geneva Press, 1977.

Owens, Milton E., Jr., ed. *Outstanding Black Sermons: Volume 3*. Reprint, Valley Forge, PA: Judson Press, 2000.

Sims, Darryl D., ed. *Sound the Trumpet: Messages to Empower African American Men*. Valley Forge, PA: Judson Press, 2002.

Smith, J. Alfred, ed. *Outstanding Black Sermons*. Reprint, Valley Forge, PA: Judson Press, 2000.

Stewart, Warren Sr. *Interpreting God's Word in Black Preaching*. Valley Forge, PA: Judson Press, 1984.

Taylor, Edward L., compiler. *The Words of Gardner Taylor: Volumes 1–6*. Valley Forge, PA: Judson Press, 2001.

Thomas, Gerald Lamont. *African American Preaching: The Contribution of Dr. Gardner C. Taylor*. New York City: Peter Lang Publishers, 2004.

Thomas, Frank A., and Martha Simmons, eds. *I Feel My Help: African American Preaching 1645–2004*. New York: Norton, forthcoming 2006.

Thomas, Frank A. *They Like to Never Quit Praisin' God: The Role of Celebration in Preaching*. Cleveland: Pilgrim Press, 1997.

Thomas, Walter S., ed. *Outstanding Black Sermons: Volume 4*. Valley Forge, PA: Judson Press, 2001.

Warren, Mervyn A. *King Came Preaching: The Pulpit Power of Dr. Martin Luther King Jr.* Downers Grove, IL: InterVarsity Press, 2001.

The Voices and Struggles of Women Preachers: These books deal with the distinctive challenges and experiences of women in the pulpit, as well as the diversity of forms and voices among women preachers.

Brekus, Catherine Anne. *Strangers and Pilgrims: Female Preaching in America, 1740–1845*. Chapel Hill: University of North Carolina, 1998.

Brown, Teresa L. Fry. *Weary Throats and New Songs: Black Women Proclaiming God's Word*. Nashville: Abingdon, 2003.

Childers, Jana, ed. *Birthing the Sermon: Women Preachers on the Creative Process*. St. Louis: Chalice Press, 2001.

Collier-Thomas, Bettye. *Daughters of Thunder: Black Women Preachers and Their Sermons 1850–1979*. San Francisco: Jossey-Bass, 1998.

Crotwell, Helen Gray, ed. *Women and the Word: Sermons*. Philadelphia: Fortress Press, 1978.

Farmer, David Albert, and Edwina Hunter, eds. *And Blessed Is She: Sermons by Women*. San Francisco: Harper and Row, 1990.

Kienzle, Beverly Mayne, and Pamela Walker, eds. *Women Preachers and Prophets through Two Millennia*. Berkeley: University of California Press, 1998.

LaRue, Cleophus, ed. *This Is My Story: Testimonies and Sermons of Black Women in Ministry*. Louisville: Westminster/John Knox Press, 2005.

McGee, Lee. *Wrestling with the Patriarchs: Retrieving Women's Voices in Preaching*. Nashville: Abingdon, 1996.

Mitchell, Ella Pearson, ed. *Women: To Preach or Not to Preach*. Valley Forge, PA: Judson Press, 1991.

———, ed. *Those Preaching Women: Sermons by Black*

Women Preachers, Volumes 1–4. Valley Forge, PA: Judson Press, 1985, 1988, 1996, 2004.

Noren, Carol M. *The Woman in the Pulpit.* Nashville: Abingdon, 1991.

Smith, Christine. *Weaving the Sermon: Preaching in a Feminist Perspective.* Louisville: Westminster/John Knox Press, 1989.

Trible, Phyllis. *Texts of Terror: Literary-Feminist Readings of Biblical Narratives.* Philadelphia: Fortress Press, 1984.

Zink-Sawyer, Beverly. *From Preachers to Suffragists: Woman's Rights and Religious Conviction in the Lives of Three Nineteenth-Century American Clergywomen.* Louisville: Westminster/John Knox Press, 2003.

Specific Topics in Preaching: These books concentrate either on particular themes to be preached or on particular groups of persons to whom sermons are directed.

Black, Kathy. *A Healing Homiletics: Preaching and Disability.* Nashville: Abingdon, 1996.

Burghardt, Walter. *Preaching the Just Word.* New Haven, CT: Yale University Press, 1996.

Brueggemann, Walter. *The Threat of Life: Sermons on Pain, Power and Weakness.* Minneapolis: Fortress Press, 1996.

Gonzalez, Justo L., and Catherine G. Gonzalez. *Liberation Preaching: The Pulpit and the Oppressed.* Nashville: Abingdon, 1980.

Hewitt, Beth Edington. *Captivating Children's Sermons.* Grand Rapids: Baker, 2004.

Jensen, Richard A. *Envisioning the Word: The Use of*

Visual Images in Preaching. Philadelphia: Fortress Press, 2004.

Johnston, Robert K. *Reel Spirituality: Theology and Film in Dialogue*. Grand Rapids: Baker, 2000.

LeQuire, Stan L. *The Best Preaching on Earth: Sermons on Caring for Creation*. Valley Forge, PA: Judson Press, 1996.

Mitchell, Jolyn P. *Visually Speaking: Radio and the Renaissance of Preaching*. Louisville: Westminster/John Knox Press, 1999.

Resner, Andre, ed. *Just Preaching: Prophetic Voices for Economic Justice*. St. Louis: Chalice Press, 2003.

Stone, Bryan P. *Faith and Film: Theological Themes at the Cinema*. St. Louis: Chalice Press, 2000.

Troeger, Thomas H. *Preaching and Worship*. St. Louis: Chalice Press, 2003.

Webb, Joseph M. *Comedy and Preaching*. St. Louis: Chalice Press, 1998.

Technical Resources for Sermon Preparation: These books offer preachers assistance in the analysis of the text, the study of the original languages, and the geographical and cultural issues that impact the passage. These books are basically research tools.

Aland, Kurt, et al., eds. *Greek New Testament*. N.p.: United Bible Societies, 1968.

Alexander, T. Desmond, and David W. Baker, eds. *Dictionary of the Old Testament: Pentateuch*. Downers Grove, IL: InterVarsity Press, 2003.

Arndt, William F., and F. Wilbur Gingrich, eds. *A Greek/*

English Lexicon of the New Testament. Chicago: The University of Chicago Press, 1974.

Arnold, Bill T., and Bryan E. Beyer. *Encountering the Old Testament*. Grand Rapids: Baker, 1999.

Botterweck, G. Johannes, and Helmer Ringgren, eds. *Theological Dictionary of the Old Testament, Volumes 1–3*. Grand Rapids: Eerdmans, 1974.

Brown, Francis, S. R. Driver, and Charles Briggs, eds. *Hebrew and English Lexicon of the Old Testament*. London: Oxford Press, 1968.

Crim, Keith R., and George A. Buttrick. *The Interpreter's Dictionary of the Bible, Volumes 1–5*. Nashville: Abingdon, 1962.

Elwell, Walter A., and Robert Yarbrough. *Encountering the New Testament*. Grand Rapids: Baker, 1999.

Green, Jay P., Sr., ed. *Interlinear Greek-English New Testament*. Grand Rapids: Baker, 1996.

Kittel, Gerhard, ed. *Theological Dictionary of the New Testament: Volumes 1–10*. Grand Rapids: Eerdmans, 1977.

Kittel, Rudolf, ed. *Biblia Hebraica*. Germany: Wurttembergische Biblelanstalt Stuttgart, 1937.

May, Herbert G., ed. *Oxford Bible Atlas*. New York: Oxford, 1974.

Miller, Madeleine S., and J. Lane Miller, eds. *Harper's Bible Dictionary*. New York: Harper and Row, 1961.

Richardson, Alan, ed. *A Theological Word Book of the Bible*. New York: Collier Books, 1962.

Strong, James, ed. *The New Strong's Exhaustive Concordance of the Bible*. Nashville: Thomas Nelson, 1995.

Webb, Joseph M., and Robert Kysar. *Greek for Preachers*. St. Louis: Chalice Press, 2002.

Whitaker, Richard E., ed. *The Eerdmans Analytical*

Concordance of the RSV of the Bible. Grand Rapids: Eerdmans, 1988.

Zodhiates, Spiro, ed. *The Hebrew-Greek Key Study Bible.* Iowa Falls: World Publishers, 1988.

Commentary Series: This is a list of the multivolume commentary series that are most widely used. It must be remembered that various commentary series reflect widely different theological perspectives. This list attempts to reflect that diversity.

Anderson, Francis I., and David Noel Freedman, eds. *The Anchor Bible Series.* New York: Doubleday Books.

Atkinson, David, J. A. Motyer, and John R. W. Stott, eds. *The Bible Speaks Today.* Downers Grove, IL: InterVarsity Press.

Keck, Leander E., series ed. *The New Interpreter's Bible*, 12 volumes. Nashville: Abingdon.

Mays, James L., series ed. *Interpretation: A Bible Commentary for Teaching and Preaching,* 43 volumes. Louisville: Westminster/John Knox Press.

Miller, Patrick, and David Bartlett, eds. *Westminster Bible Companion.* Louisville: Westminster/John Knox Press.

Morris, Leon, ed. *Tyndale New Testament Commentary Series.* Grand Rapids: Eerdmans.

Osborne, Grant R., ed. *The IVP New Testament Commentary Series.* Downers Grove, IL: InterVarsity Press.

Various, eds. *Abingdon New Testament Commentaries.* Nashville: Abingdon.

Various, eds. *Abingdon Old Testament Commentaries.* Nashville: Abingdon.

Various, eds. *Word Biblical Commentary.* Dallas: Word.

Wright, G. Ernest, et al., eds. *The Old Testament Library.* Philadelphia: Westminster Press, Philadelphia.

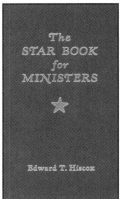